How To Detect And Prevent Business Fraud

HOW TO DETECT AND PREVENT BUSINESS FRAUD

by

W. STEVE ALBRECHT, Ph.D., C.P.A.
Institute of Professional Accountancy
Brigham Young University

MARSHALL B. ROMNEY, Ph.D., C.P.A.
Institute of Professional Accountancy
Brigham Young University

DAVID J. CHERRINGTON, D.B.A.
Department of Organizational Behavior
Brigham Young University

I. REED PAYNE, Ph.D.
Department of Psychology
Brigham Young University

ALLAN V. ROE, Ph.D.
Prison Psychologist
Utah State Prison

PRENTICE-HALL, INC.
Englewood Cliffs, New Jersey

Prentice-Hall, Inc., *London*
Prentice-Hall of Australia, Pty. Ltd., *Sydney*
Prentice-Hall of Canada, Ltd., *Toronto*
Prentice-Hall of India Private Ltd., *New Delhi*
Prentice-Hall of Japan, Inc., *Tokyo*
Prentice Hall of Southeast Asia, Pte. Ltd., *Singapore*
Whitehall Books, Ltd., Wellington, *New Zealand*

©1982, by

Prentice-Hall, Inc.

Library of Congress Cataloging in Publication Data
Main entry under title:

How to detect and prevent business fraud.

   Bibliography: p.
   Includes index.
   1. Fraud.   2. White collar crimes.   3. Business—
Security measures.   4. Fraud—United States.   5. White
collar crimes—United States.   I. Albrecht, W. Steve.
HV6691.H68   658.4′73   81-12015
ISBN 0-13-404707-9   AACR2

Printed in the United States of America

A WORD FROM THE AUTHORS

This book will help auditors and managers detect and deter fraud. The major causes of fraud are explained, fraud perpetrators are profiled, and strategies for uncovering and eliminating fraud are analyzed. The costs of fraud are enormous, and the occurrence of fraud has increased rapidly. It has been estimated that fraud and white-collar crime costs $200 billion per year in the United States alone—an average of $1,000 per person. Fraud has been referred to as a growth industry, the crime of the 80s, the royal ripoff, and a potential threat to our active economy.

The recommendations contained in the following chapters culminate a three-year study of fraud funded by a grant from the Big-8 accounting firm of Peat, Marwick, Mitchell and Company. The causes of fraud were derived from an extensive review of thousands of pages of literature and many hours of personal interviews. The suggested methods for reducing fraud were gleaned from numerous sources including: actual company practices, books on fraud, and suggestions from such organizations as the FBI, the Securities and Exchange Commission, and major accounting firms.

This book is divided into three sections. Section I, comprising Chapters 1 and 2, outlines the problem of fraud and its background. Section II, comprising Chapters 3 through 6, describes strategies for reducing management fraud, and Section III, comprising Chapters 7 through 10, presents strategies for reducing employee fraud.

The following benefits demonstrate the value of this book:

- In *Chapter 1*, the different types of fraud are illustrated

5

with factual cases. Statistics demonstrate the seriousness and extensiveness of fraud, and reasons why auditors and managers must make concerted efforts to control it.

- In *Chapter 2*, the major causes of fraud are identified and a framework for understanding why it occurs is presented. The importance of developing an early warning system (red flags and checklists) is discussed and major theories of fraud are reviewed.
- *Chapter 3* describes situational pressures contributing to management fraud. Financial pressures, company limitations, economic conditions, and legal difficulties that encourage fraud are explained and documented with 72 major cases of fraud.
- *Chapter 4* describes opportunities that make management fraud easier to commit, such as related-party transactions, an inadequate internal accounting system, frequent changes in auditors or legal counsel, and an inadequate internal audit team.
- Evidences of low personal integrity that should be investigated are described in *Chapter 5*, for example, individuals who lack a personal code of ethics or have a questionable or criminal background.
- *Chapter 6* contains a detailed risk evaluation questionnaire that can be used in preventing and detecting fraud.
- *Chapter 7* describes the kinds of situational pressures that need to be recognized to reduce employee fraud, such as inadequate income, living beyond one's means, gambling, stock market speculation, and unreasonable social expectations.
- *Chapter 8* describes how to make employee fraud less convenient by eliminating opportunities, such as close associations with suppliers, the absence of mandatory vacations, lack of internal security, and inadequate personnel screening policies.
- Recommendations for hiring persons of high personal integrity are contained in *Chapter 9*, with specific sug-

gestions about the use of polygraph tests, paper and pencil tests, and pre-employment interviews.

- *Chapter 10* contains a summary of management strategies for reducing fraud and an analysis of social conditions that encourage fraud. This concluding chapter illustrates why the war on fraud requires a concerted effort by auditors, managers, and other social institutions.

- For those who are interested in the research foundations, *Appendices A and B* describe the research methodology and a more detailed review of the literature. The traditional explanations of crime are summarized to show why a better framework explaining fraud is needed.

- A study comparing fraud perpetrators with other property criminals and college students is reported in *Appendix C*. This study illustrates how fraud perpetrators are more like common citizens than like other criminals.

- *Appendix D* includes tables which cross-reference the red flags with 52 past cases of fraud.

AUTHORS' RESEARCH NOTE

Most of the personal names in this book have been changed to avoid unnecessary embarrassment. Many of the cases are well known and have been widely publicized in newspapers, magazines, journals and other media. The purpose of this book is not to expose or sensationalize fraud, but rather to document it and illustrate some of the practices, situations, or characteristics that appear to be red flags in fraud detection and prevention.

The research on which this book is based was funded by a grant from Peat, Marwick, Mitchell and Company Foundation. We are grateful for their generous financial support and personal encouragement. Nevertheless, the views expressed herein are those of the authors and do not necessarily reflect the views of Peat, Marwick, Mitchell and Company Foundation. We are also grateful to Donn Parker (SRI International) for allowing us access to his personal records, and to the AICPA (*Journal of*

Accountancy), the NAA (*Management Accounting*), the California District Attorney's Association (*Prosecutor's Brief*) and *U.S. News and World Report*, for giving us permission to use the parts of this book that were previously published as research in those publications. In addition, some of the results of the study on which this book is based have been published as a chapter in *Management Fraud: Dectection and Deterrence*, published by Petrocelli Books, Inc. We express our appreciation to them for allowing us to use the material in this book. Finally, we appreciate the extensive labors of our research assistants and typists in the North Word Processing Center, Brigham Young University.

W. Steve Albrecht
Marshall B. Romney
David J. Cherrington
I. Reed Payne
Allan V. Roe

CONTENTS

How To Detect
And Prevent
Business Fraud

SECTION I

THE PROBLEM AND ITS BACKGROUND

1

THE
ROYAL
RIPOFF

Johnson, Jackson, and Jeffrey were the auditors for the Mayberry Corporation, a conglomerate with about $1 billion in sales.[1] They had audited the company for three years, each time giving an unqualified opinion. This year, however, something was different. Their observation of inventory had revealed no serious shortages and yet it seemed dramatically overstated. Why would their inventory increase five-fold in one year? Suspecting something was awry, the auditors performed some "midnight auditing." Their investigation revealed that the sheet metal inventory was grossly overstated. The auditors had almost been deceived.

Management had falsified the inventory by preparing fictitious records. Their people had prepared inventory tags and delivered them to Johnson, Jackson, and Jeffrey's auditors. The auditors had verified the amount of inventory shown on the tags and had deposited them in a box in the conference room they used during the audit. A manager had then added spurious tags to the box at night. However, since there was very little time to fabricate a large number of reasonable tags, some were made to show rolls of sheet metal weighing as much as 50,000 pounds. The manager had also substituted new inventory reconciliation lists to conform with the total of the valid and spurious tags.

The magnitude of the fraud was discovered when Johnson, Jackson, and Jeffrey performed some analytical tests. First, they converted the purported $30 million of sheet metal stock

---

[1] While the names used in this book are fictitious and the facts are sometimes stated rather simply, most scenarios are based on actual frauds. Details of this case were provided by L. B. Sawyer, Internal Auditor and Insight Services, Consultants, who detect management fraud.

into cubic feet. Then they determined the volume of the warehouse that was supposed to contain the inventory. At best, it could have only contained one-half the reported amount—it was far too small to house the total. Next, they examined the inventory tags and found that some rolls of sheet metal were supposed to weigh 50,000 pounds. However, none of the fork lifts that were supposed to move the inventory could possibly lift over 3,000 pounds. Finally, the auditors verified the reported inventory purchases and found purchase orders supporting an inventory of about 30 million pounds. Yet, the reported amount was 60 million pounds.

Faced with this evidence, management admitted that they had grossly overstated the value of the inventory to show increased profits and agreed to write the inventory down from $30 million to $7 million. Management had previously forecast increased earnings, and without the overstatement, their earnings would have fallen far short of their target. As for Johnson, Jackson, and Jeffrey, they had avoided a potentially damaging lawsuit as well as public exposure and embarrassment.

Janet D. was hired to assist several employees in the office of a wholesale candy and tobacco distributor.[2] Although not highly educated, she learned the office procedures well and often worked as a substitute cashier. When the regular cashier resigned, Janet D. knew the bookkeeping system so well that she was promoted to cashier.

It was on her 19th birthday, she later told investigators, that she first took money from her employer. The $300 she took was used to pay for an abortion the following weekend.

Several months after the illegal operation, Janet met Alfred G. at a teenage hangout. He had a police record, was out of a job, and needed money for car payments. He insisted Janet get some money for him, or his car would be repossessed. For some time she resisted, but then gave in and took several hundred dollars more. After this, it was easy for Alfred G. to keep up the pressure. Janet provided the money for utility and rent payments on his apartment, gave him cash, and bought him expensive gifts, including a diamond ring, a stereo

---

[2] The source of this scenario is "The Forty Thieves," published by the U.S. Fidelity and Guaranty Company, 1970.

set, and a watch. They often took pleasure jaunts together, such as to the "drag races" at a nearby city. On these excursions, Alfred G. later bragged, they always traveled "first class" and Janet paid all of the bills for hotel rooms, transportation, meals, and entertainment.

Janet's employer had a triplicate system of invoices—the duplicate copy going to the customer as he picked up his order, the original copy to a clerical employee, and the triplicate being put in the cash drawer along with the cash or check in payment of the order. However, Janet was often allowed to handle both the original and triplicate invoices. She would take money from the cash drawer in the amount of an invoice, and then destroy both copies of the invoice. She also substituted some customers' checks for money that she took from the drawer. This substitution apparently led to the ultimate discovery of her embezzlement which, over a few months, amounted to over $50,000.

Shortly before she was discovered, Janet D. had told her employer that she was soon going to get married and move to another state. Before moving, however, her bubble burst. Her embezzlement was discovered and her boyfriend was charged with extortion.

Ribeye Corporation[3] was a large northwestern restaurant chain whose computerized payroll system was processed by a service bureau. At each two-week pay interval, after receiving the most current input from the payroll clerk, the service bureau would process the payroll checks for each restaurant employee. This stack of checks was then delivered to the clerk, who ran each check through a check-signer and delivered the packets of checks to each of the restaurants in the chain for distribution to the employees.

During the year, the clerk created fictitious employees. He "hired" them by manufacturing hourly time records that were added to the regular payroll data and forwarded to the service bureau. The service bureau's computer dutifully printed out paychecks for the phony employees along with those of the real ones. It was an easy task for the clerk to endorse and convert the checks to cash, using his own checking account as

---

[3] The source for this scenario is *Management World*, July 1977. (See Anderson, 1977)

a clearing-house. From time to time, he would "terminate" some of his employees and replace them with other fictitious names, but always with the same result: a fraudulent check was issued to the name of the new employee at the next regular pay interval. This computer fraud resulted in a loss of $293,000 to Ribeye Corporation.

These three cases illustrate the kind of fraud that occurs everyday in America. The first was a large management fraud that would have resulted in the overstatement of financial statements. The second was a smaller fraud perpetrated by an employee against her company and the third was a typical computer fraud. These are not isolated incidences; both the dollar amounts and the number of all three types of frauds are increasing. Consider the following statistics:

- Some 250 American companies notified the Securities and Exchange Commission in 1976 that they had made illegal or questionable payments in the United States and abroad. Some of these payments ran into the millions of dollars and involved high officials in the United States, Europe, and Japan.

- A recent scheme of kickbacks and bribes involving certain longshoremen, shipping companies, and port officials from New Orleans to Boston caused the cost of goods arriving at the ports to increase by 30 percent. It is estimated that the cost of all purchased goods is increased by 15–30 percent because of the dishonest acts of management and employees.

- During the first six months of 1979, $80 million slipped out the back doors of banks through employee fraud: more than triple the $23 million lost from bank robberies.

- Fraud was the major factor contributing to the forced closing of about 100 banks during the 1970s.

- It is estimated that total losses from white-collar crime and fraud are approximately $200 billion per year.

These estimates and statistics indicate the tremendous problems facing the business community as it attempts to cope with fraud. In fact, based on experience, one consulting firm estimates that there is more than a 50 percent chance of sizable dishonesty in any firm, and a 75 percent chance of harmful malpractice sufficient to impair the firm's profit structure. Perhaps even more startling than the increase in known incidents of fraud are the following estimates regarding undetected and unprosecuted computer fraud.

- The FBI estimates that only one percent of computer-based crimes are ever discovered.
- IBM executive, Ray Ellison (1976) stated that in a study of 339 known cases of computer-related fraud or embezzlement in the USA in 1974, 85 percent never resulted in criminal proceedings. Of the remaining 15 percent going to trial, only 20 percent received a prison sentence.

If these estimates are correct, it can be concluded that perpetrators of computer-related frauds have a 3,333 to 1 (.01 $\times$ .15 $\times$ .20) chance of successfully evading detection, prosecution, and imprisonment. These are certainly not bad odds, since the average loss for the 339 studied cases was a cool half of a million dollars. In fact, computer fraud is growing so fast that in 1979, *Time Magazine* labeled it a "growth industry."

Consider the following FBI and Justice Department estimates:

Average loss in computer-related fraud is	$500,000
Average loss in a bank fraud without a computer is	23,500
Average loss in a bank robbery is	3,200
Average loss in a burglary is	450
Average loss in an armed robbery is	250
Average loss in a larceny is	150

Donn Parker, a leading expert in computer crime, has made the following predictions for the 1980s:

- Organized crime will make its debut in computer crime.
- Organized crime will use career criminals and ex-cons trained in computer technology by prison rehabilitation programs. (Computer technology training programs are one of the most popular.)

- Organized crime will force "honest" computer personnel to help them defraud systems.

- The amount lost per incident will rise (from the present figure of $500,000).

- Professional data processing criminals will be more skilled and less likely to be detected (only 1 percent are now detected).

- Terrorist groups and unfriendly nations will use computers to wreck havoc on American business.

Average losses to shareholders and others from management fraud cases are not determinable. There are several instances involving losses of over $100 to $200 million dollars to shareholders alone. Certainly, losses from management fraud dwarf even those of computer-related crimes. It doesn't take more than a quick look at these estimates to see where the bright criminals will be spending their time in the 1980s. Both Parker's predictions and the statistics and estimates mentioned indicate why the FBI has labeled fraud and white-collar crime "The crime of the 1980s." The FBI recognizes the tremendous problems it faces; more FBI resources are now devoted to the detection of fraud and white-collar crime than any other criminal activity, with over 24 percent of their available manpower assigned to its detection (1,700 special agents at a cost of $86 million a year to U.S. taxpayers).

These statistics and illustrations show that fraud is one of the serious problems facing America today. Instances of all three types—management fraud, employee embezzlement, and computer fraud—are rapidly increasing and both auditors and managers need to be aware of their consequences and warning signals.

For the past three years, we have conducted an extensive interdisciplinary study of fraud in which we attempted to understand fraud perpetrators and their motivations, and those actions that society, managers, and auditors can take to control fraud. This book is a summary of our findings. The conclusions reported here are based on research, and the insights and recommendations are practical and easy to implement. Thus, it should help both auditors and managers to better understand, prevent, and control fraud.

Specifically, Chapter 2 discusses strategies for reducing fraud. It includes an analysis of three reasons why people commit fraud, along with a brief overview of how it can best be prevented. Section II, comprising Chapters 3 through 6, focuses on management fraud and provides recommendations for its detection and deterrence. The emphasis is on management fraud and the red flags that serve as warning signals. Chapter 3 identifies the business pressures that signal a high potential for fraud. Chapter 4 examines opportunities that make it easier for management to commit fraud, while Chapter 5 discusses the personality characteristics of management fraud perpetrators. Each of these three chapters takes one of the three causes of fraud, and (1) explains the reason why it contributes to dishonest acts, (2) identifies the factors auditors should examine in order to detect fraud, and (3) provides illustrations that show how each factor was present in major fraud cases. Chapter 6 then ties this section together by providing a checklist of questions that can be used explicitly to consider whether or not fraud exists in a company. The checklist is a risk-evaluation questionnaire that identifies specific procedures for detecting fraud.

Section III, comprised of Chapters 7 through 10, emphasizes embezzlement and computer fraud by employees. Chapter 7 identifies situational pressures that motivate employees to commit fraud, while Chapter 8 examines the company characteristics that provide opportunities for employees to more easily commit, conceal, and avoid prosecution for their dishonest acts. Chapter 9 examines those personal characteristics of employees that influence their level of honesty, and describes various ways in which the level of employee integrity can be assessed. Like Chapters 3 through 5, each chapter takes one of the causes of fraud and (1) explains how it contributes to dishonest acts, (2) identifies the factors managers need to be aware of, (3) provides illustrations showing how each factor was observed in major employee embezzlement and computer fraud cases, and (4) provides summary tables that validate the red flags. Chapter 10 then summarizes actions managers can take to reduce fraud. Personnel policies and practices are examined and their effect on reducing fraud is highlighted. Chapter 10 also includes an explanation of how society reinforces fraud.

The four appendices at the end of the book describe our research study and provide a summary of our literature review. Appendix A reviews the traditional explanations of crime and fraud. Appendix B describes our specific research methodology, Appendix C presents the results of an empirical analysis comparing the profiles of fraud perpetrators and other property offenders, while Appendix D includes charts that cross reference the red flags with the 72 major cases cited in the book.

Exhibit I is a graphical outline of the book. While we believe you will find the entire book helpful and interesting, auditors will be most interested in Chapters 1–6, while managers should find Chapters 1–2 and 7–10 most helpful.

Exhibit 1-1

Outline of the Book

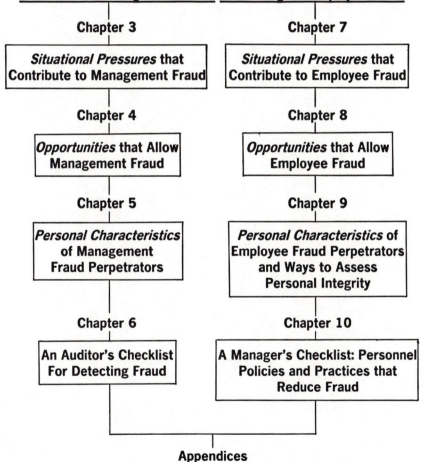

Chapter 1

Statistics on Fraud
"Why It Is So Extensive"

Chapter 2

Strategies for Reducing Fraud
Why Fraud Occurs

For Auditors: Management Fraud | **For Managers: Employee Fraud**

Chapter 3

Situational Pressures that
Contribute to Management Fraud

Chapter 7

Situational Pressures that
Contribute to Employee Fraud

Chapter 4

Opportunities that Allow
Management Fraud

Chapter 8

Opportunities that Allow
Employee Fraud

Chapter 5

Personal Characteristics
of Management
Fraud Perpetrators

Chapter 9

Personal Characteristics of
Employee Fraud Perpetrators
and Ways to Assess
Personal Integrity

Chapter 6

An Auditor's Checklist
For Detecting Fraud

Chapter 10

A Manager's Checklist: Personnel
Policies and Practices that
Reduce Fraud

Appendices

Appendix A: Traditional Explanations of Crime
Appendix B: The Research Methodology
Appendix C: Profile of Fraud Perpetrators
Appendix D: Fraud Validation Tables

2

STRATEGIES FOR REDUCING FRAUD

Reasonable strategies for reducing fraud must be based upon an accurate diagnosis of the causes of fraud. The various explanations, however, have not been entirely consistent. Fraud has been studied by numerous individuals in various disciplines, including psychology, sociology, criminology, and business. Generally, researchers in each discipline have described fraud from their own perspectives, emphasizing different aspects of the problem. In the past, the following types of questions about fraud have been addressed.

Which personality traits or individual characteristics contribute to fraud? To what extent do environmental variables and social forces influence the commission of fraud? Is honesty a general personality trait or is it specific to each situation? How is honesty learned, and are people consistently honest? Can general theories of criminality and deviant behavior explain fraud? The following is a brief review of some of the major explanations of crime. This review helps to explain the causes of fraud shown in the model at the end of the chapter.

PSYCHOLOGICAL EXPLANATIONS OF CRIME

Historically, psychologists have developed two major explanations of crime. One explanation comes from psychoanalytic theory, while the other comes from learning theory. The psychoanalytic theory suggests that criminals (including fraud perpetrators) behave as they do because they are in some way "sick" or "maladjusted." According to Sigmund Freud, such sickness can be caused by two possible malfunctions in the individual's development. The first cause of fraud can be attrib-

uted to a person's id—one of the three parts of the personality
—which strives to satisfy basic needs and desires. Criminal acts
are sometimes attributed to the failure of individuals to control
the raw, uninhibited impulses of the id. They steal and commit
other crimes because these actions are the easiest means of
satisfying uncontrolled impulses and basic desires. Since most
of the id's influence is from the subconscious or the unconscious, fraud perpetrators are seldom aware of the real influences on or causes of their criminal activity.

The second malfunction contributing to fraud is attributed
to the superego—another part of the personality. The superego, often equated with the "conscience," is the motivational
force that keeps people from committing antisocial acts. This
explanation suggests that fraud results from an underdeveloped conscience stemming from a lack of parental identification and social training. People with underdeveloped con-
sciences have not acquired strong superegos to help them
channel their energies into socially approved activities, so they
do not feel guilty when they commit antisocial acts. Since their
acts of dishonesty do not create feelings of guilt or remorse,
they can be expected to commit fraud whenever there is an
opportunity to do so with little chance of being caught.

A second major psychological explanation of fraud comes
from learning theory which suggests that fraud, like all behavior, is determined by one's environment. According to this explanation, which is based on the theory of operant conditioning, individuals will do what their environment reinforces
or rewards them for doing. If they are reinforced for being
honest, they will be honest. If dishonesty is reinforced, they
will be dishonest. Most fraudulent behavior is supposedly
learned by operant conditioning, where behavior is influenced
by the kinds of rewards and punishments that are associated
with it. If the consequences of an act are desirable, the person
will probably continue to perform that act. If the consequences are undesirable, the probability of doing it again is reduced. Unfortunately, crime often pays, and each time it pays,
the related behavior is reinforced. Criminal behaviors are also
reinforced by the removal of painful stimuli, such as impending debts. A perpetrator's pro-social behaviors are weakened when he is punished for these behaviors (such as when
his friends make fun of him for passing up an easy buck or

when he reports a fraudulent act). Under this theory, perpetrators become involved in crime after being reinforced for
some small, illegal act that encourages them to do more.

In some cases, reinforcements or punishments do not have
to be experienced directly; they can be experienced vicariously. The potential perpetrator of fraud can see others getting
rewards for their crimes, then imitate their behavior. Or, the
perpetrators might imagine themselves carrying out the criminal act and getting the reward; this fantasy reinforces them
and increases the probability of their actually committing the
crime. In most crimes, criminals are reinforced by money or
goods that can be exchanged for other forms of reinforcement.
They may also be reinforced by revenge, power, control, or
even social approval.

SOCIOLOGICAL EXPLANATIONS OF CRIME

Sociological explanations of fraud are quite similar to
learning theory. The two most well-known explanations are
Sutherland's "differential association" theory (Sutherland and
Cressey, 1978) and Cressey's "nonshareable need" theory
(1953). While specifically addressing white-collar crime, both
of these explanations provide considerable insight into the motivations of fraud perpetrators.

In Sutherland's view, criminal behavior is linked to a person's association with a criminal environment. People encounter various social influences throughout their lives. Some
individuals have social interactions with individuals having
criminalistic tendencies and so become criminals as a consequence of this association.

The major elements in Sutherland's differential association
theory can be summarized as follows (Sutherland and Cressey,
1978):

1. Criminal behavior is learned; it is not inherited, and the
person who is not already trained in crime does not invent
criminal behavior.

2. Criminal behavior is learned through interaction with
other people, through the processes of verbal communication
and example.

3. The principle learning of criminal behavior occurs with intimate personal groups.

4. The learning of crime includes learning the techniques of committing the crime, and the motives, drives, rationalizations, and attitudes that accompany it.

5. A person becomes delinquent because of an excess of definitions (or personal reactions) favorable to the violation of the law over definitions unfavorable to the violation of the law.

The essence of Sutherland's argument is that criminal behavior is engaged in by persons who have accumulated enough feelings and rationalizations in favor of law violation to outweigh their pro-social definitions. Criminal behavior is learned and will occur when the perceived rewards for criminal behavior exceed the rewards of lawful behavior.

A related but alternative sociological theory of fraud was proposed by Cressey (1953). He defined the problem as a "violation of a position of financial trust" that the person originally took in good faith. To quote from his work:

> Trusted persons become trust violators when they conceive of themselves as having a financial problem which is nonsharable, are aware that this problem can be secretly resolved by violation of the position of financial trust, and are able to apply to their conduct in that situation verbalizations which enable them to adjust their conceptions of themselves as users of the entrusted funds or property.

There must be (1) a nonsharable problem, (2) an opportunity for trust violation, and (3) a set of rationalizations that define the behavior as appropriate in a given situation. None of these elements alone would be sufficient to result in embezzlement; all three elements must be present. Evidence for Cressey's theory rested on in-depth interviews with those convicted of trust violations. He claimed that all of the cases he studied conformed to the three-step process.

MORAL DEVELOPMENT EXPLANATIONS

In addition to psychological and sociological explanations, research in moral development provides considerable insights into the possible causes of fraud. Honesty is a "moral" behavior. Management fraud, embezzlement, kickbacks, bribes, and theft are all forms of dishonest behavior. When an executive misrepresents a business transaction or steals from a company, he is behaving dishonestly. When a computer technician manipulates the computer systems to place a fraction of a cent from each employee's payroll calculation into a hidden account that he can withdraw from, he is behaving dishonestly. When a purchasing agent receives kickbacks by arranging to make purchase orders and payments for more merchandise than is received, he is behaving dishonestly.

The moral development literature makes several contributions toward understanding fraud. First, it helps solve the dilemma of whether or not honesty is a general personality trait: whether or not individuals are either wholly honest or dishonest. Second, it explains why individuals behave honestly in some situations and dishonestly in others. Third, it helps explain which forces contribute to the development of honesty and how honesty can be taught.

Some researchers have argued that moral behavior is *situationally specific*; people will behave according to how they have been taught to act in each particular environment. This means that honesty is situational. People will be honest in some situations and dishonest in others. People will commit fraud when it is convenient, or when they have done it before in similar situations.

The opposite of situational honesty is the idea of *general* honesty, which claims that individuals acquire an overall personality or character trait of "honesty," and behave consistently at all times and in different situations. Therefore, a meticulously honest person should be honest in all situations regardless of the temptations, and a person who tends to be dishonest should behave dishonestly whenever it is expedient.

Moral development research suggests that the truth lies somewhere between these two extremes. For some individuals, honesty is a situationally specific behavior; but for other individuals, it is a general personality trait. It appears that the difference between general honesty and situationally specific honesty results from two characteristics of a person's relationship with other important individuals, such as parents or an employer. First is the degree of consistency in administering positive reinforcement for honest behavior and punishment for dishonest behavior. Second is the verbal labeling of situations to develop a general definition of what is honest and what is dishonest. All situations requiring honesty need to be consistently defined to evoke consistent responses of honesty. Thus, if parents and managers consistently reward and encourage honesty and give verbal labels to honest and dishonest behavior, children and employees will most likely develop a general character trait of honesty. However, if parents and managers simply punish or reward moral behavior, without giving it a label or explaining the principle, or if the standard of honesty is inconsistent, children and employees will most likely be inconsistent in their moral behavior. For example, condemning dishonesty in one situation, such as stealing money, but encouraging it in another situation, such as cheating on expense reimbursement forms, will lead to situational honesty.

The research on moral development helps to explain why a business executive would not necessarily behave honestly in all situations. An executive who would not think of manipulating stock prices, financial reports, or accounting procedures might willingly participate in an illegal kickback scheme. Executives will behave honestly in all situations only if they have learned to correctly identify and label the honest responses, and if they have been consistently rewarded for honesty and punished for dishonesty. The general honesty of employees is thus determined by the developmental experiences they have had, both as children and during their earlier work experiences. For this reason, it is important that organizations clearly define for their employees *what* is dishonest behavior. Also, swift and predictable consequences should be widely publicized and judiciously executed.

CAUSES OF FRAUD

The research on moral development, along with psychological and sociological explanations of crime, greatly contributed to our understanding of fraud. However, the explanation of fraud delineated in this book was derived largely from examining cases of fraud rather than from the theoretical literature. The focus of our three-year study was on the following research objectives:

1) To conduct an extensive review of all fraud-related literature;

2) To identify individual, organizational, and societal factors that suggest a high probability of fraud;

3) To validate these factors by comparing them to past cases of fraud; and

4) To organize the factors into early-warning systems that can be used to detect and deter fraud.

To investigate the causes of fraud, we reviewed over 1,500 references on fraud, including books, journal and magazine articles, monographs, newspaper citations, and unpublished documents. Numerous fraud perpetrators and victims of fraud (representatives from both large and small corporations, and members of auditing firms, as well as probationed, parolled, and incarcerated perpetrators) were personally interviewed. Contacts were made with 55 organizations (such as the FBI, the SEC, and investigative agencies) concerned with understanding either the detection, deterrence, prosecution or punishment of fraud. Various other sources were also reviewed, such as Donn Parker's (SRI International) extensive files on computer-fraud, plus numerous probation, parole, and prison records.

As the various sources were examined, a comprehensive list of all variables that appeared to influence or be associated with the perpetration of fraud was compiled. In total, 82 fraud-related variables were identified. These variables, which we call "red flags," were classified into three major categories representing the forces that influence the decision to commit or not commit fraud (see Exhibit 2-1). We concluded that it was the combination of these three forces that produces a fraudulent act, and have labeled them:

Situational pressures,
Opportunities to commit fraud, and
Personal integrity (character).

Situational pressures refer to the immediate pressures individuals experience within their environment. The most overwhelming pressures are usually high personal debts or financial losses. Low incomes contribute to financial pressures, but gambling, stock market speculation, and expensive habits or tastes are generally the most significant causes of intense financial pressures. Situational pressures can also be generated by strong peer group influences and even by official company directives to achieve unrealistic performance objectives at any cost. Occasionally, situational pressures encourage individuals to commit fraud *for* the company rather than against the company, such as the threat of losing a business license, delisting from a stock exchange, or having a cash shortage.

The opportunities to commit fraud refer to opportunities that individuals create for themselves, as well as opportunities created by the company through careless internal controls. For example, individuals can create opportunities to commit fraud by increasing their knowledge of the company's operations, by advancing to a position of trust, and by being the only person who knows a particular procedure, such as modifying the computer programs. A company can increase the opportunities for employee fraud by allowing related party transactions, by having a complex business structure, by using several different auditing or legal firms, or by having a very weak system of internal controls. Anything that contributes to the capability of perpetrating or hiding a fraud increases the opportunities for it.

Personal integrity refers to the personal code of ethical behavior each person adopts. While this factor appears to be a straightforward determination of whether the person is honest or dishonest, research on moral development (reviewed in Chapter 9 and Appendix A) indicates that the issue is more complex. Some individuals have developed a general trait of honesty that we call high personal integrity. These individuals would normally be expected to act honestly at all times, unless the situational pressures or opportunities to be dishonest were extremely strong. Individuals with low personal integrity may or may not behave honestly, depending on the situation. There may be certain situations in which they consistently behave honestly, but their honesty does not generalize to other situations and is not internalized as a personal value. Their behavior is influenced more by the situation: the opportunity to be dishonest, the probable gain from cheating, the likelihood of getting caught, the severity of the punishment, and the perceived need for more money. Most individuals are between these two extremes. They generally believe in honesty, but can be tempted by convenient opportunities and intense situational pressures.

Exhibit 2-1 suggests that the decision to commit fraud is determined by the interaction of all three forces. A useful way to visualize the interaction is to picture a balance scale with three connecting bars at the top. Each of the three connected bars has a weight that can move independently of the other weights, in either direction. Thus, the combination of the three continua (or bars), along with the locations and sizes of the three weights, determines to which side the scale will be tilted.

Exhibit 2-1

Fraud: Three Key Variables

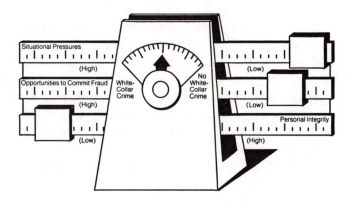

Similarly, these three forces interact to determine whether the person will or will not commit fraud. A person with a high level of personal integrity and no opportunity or pressure to commit fraud will most likely behave honestly. However, fraud becomes more likely as individuals with less personal integrity are placed in situations with increasing pressures and greater opportunities to commit fraud.

In this additive model, all of the variables contributing to fraud accumulate in each case until the force or weight is sufficient to result in a fraudulent act taking place. For example, fraud could theoretically occur under any situation if a person is motivated enough, even in the absence of outward opportunities or pressures. More likely, a situational pressure at a personal level, such as a debt or loss, would have to be combined with a predisposition to partial dishonesty in order for a crime to take place. Pressures at the organizational level, such as others who have cheated or a lack of accounting controls, would also increase the likelihood for fraud. Opportunities in general, or a specific opportunity in an individual case, increases the potential for fraud. Further removed but still relevant are the societal variables that may provide conducive attitudes, such as the rationale for a double standard (one at home, another at work). Lack of immediate punishment or absence of threat may influence taking a risk and being dishonest. If the individual has a strong, generalized honesty characteristic, he may theoretically withstand the cumulative weight of all the variables described, although some might argue that "every person has a price."

To validate the red flag list and show that these factors were indeed related to fraud, 52 past cases of fraud were studied. Information on the cases came from the publicly available literature.[1] In gathering information about the cases, an extensive search was conducted to identify all published accounts of the frauds, and over 2,000 separate citations were found and reviewed. The case information was carefully analyzed to determine which of the 82 red flags appeared to be present in the cases. The result was that every red flag could be associated with at least one case and no case was free from red-flag warning signals. In fact, 20 of the red flags were associated with at least 20 different cases, and 19 of the cases had at least 21 red-flag warnings. Fifty-one red flags were associated with the major Equity Funding' fraud case.

To develop early warning systems, the red flags were segregated into those most closely associated with employee fraud and those most closely associated with management fraud. Once classified, fraud risk evaluation checklists were developed. These checklists are included in Chapters 6 and 10 of this book.

Thus, our research findings are consistent with theories of psychology, sociology, and moral development. Furthermore, the model derived from this research can be used effectively to detect and deter fraud. We believe that this combination of methodologically sound research, along with the resulting applicability, can make a tremendous difference in efforts to understand fraud perpetrators and reduce fraud in a firm. While we concentrate only on the practical side of fraud detection and deterrence in the remainder of the book, we hope that you see the theoretical base upon which our conclusions and recommendations are founded. Appendices A, B, and C contain more detailed reviews of both prior fraud and criminality theories, and our research methodology.

---

[1] Appendix B contains a complete list of these cases.

Section II

STRATEGIES FOR REDUCING MANAGEMENT FRAUD

3

SITUATIONAL PRESSURES CONTRIBUTING TO MANAGEMENT FRAUD

Chapter 3 Explains:

- Company financial pressures that can lead to fraud.
- Company limitations that can lead to fraud.
- Business decisions that can lead to fraud.
- External economic conditions that can lead to fraud.
- Legal difficulties that can lead to fraud.

T his chapter discusses situational pressures that confront companies and may cause their management to perpetrate frauds on the companies' behalf. Because it is management that is usually involved in these types of frauds, auditors and regulators should find the contents of this chapter especially useful.

Kapnick (1976) indicated that if auditors are to detect fraud, they must have a skeptical attitude and be alert to the environment in which fraud can occur. Many of the red flags listed in this chapter spotlight impending financial problems that might cause corporate bankruptcy, the loss of corporate prestige, position, or power, or some other condition that might affect the ability of a company to continue as a going concern. A total of 25 situational pressures that might contribute to management fraud are explained in this chapter. Table 1 in Appendix D shows which company pressures are associated with the 52 fraud cases we reviewed. This chapter discusses the following company pressures:

1. Heavy investments or losses
2. Insufficient working capital
3. High debt
4. Reduced ability to acquire credit
5. Profit squeeze (costs and expenses rising higher and faster than sales and revenues)
6. Restrictive loan agreements
7. Progressive deterioration in the quality of corporate earnings
8. Urgent need for favorable earnings (to support the high price of stock, to meet earnings forecast, etc.)
9. Need to gloss over a temporarily bad situation (in order to maintain management position and prestige)
10. Unmarketable collateral
11. Dependence on only one or two products
12. Excess capacity
13. Severe obsolescence
14. Long business cycle
15. Existence of revocable and possibly imperiled licenses (especially when necessary for the continuation of business)
16. Extremely rapid expansion
17. Unfavorable economic conditions within an industry
18. Difficulty in collecting receivables
19. Unusually heavy competition
20. Significant reduction in sales backlogs indicating future sales decline
21. Pressure to merge
22. Sizable inventory increase without comparable sales increases
23. Significant tax adjustments or changes
24. Significant litigation (especially between stockholders and management)
25. Suspension or delisting from a stock exchange

HEAVY INVESTMENTS OR LOSSES

One motive management might have for fraud is the need to support unprofitable ventures (Krause, 1965). An example is the Standard Life and Accident Company (SLAC) and its parent Standard Life Corporation. SLAC had a number of subsidiaries that were losing money. One, Gulf South, accumulated losses of $5.2 million in the five years ending in 1970. Another particularly disastrous investment for SLAC was its Aunt Tilly's Brewery subsidiary in Puerto Rico. Aunt Tilly's never realized a profit, and by 1971 had accumulated losses of $5.3 million. To conceal this losing venture, Aunt Tilly's was transferred to an entity called Carolina Investment Company, which was a subsidiary of SLAC: a fact which was not disclosed. SLAC then made loans to Carolina and carried them as accounts receivable. Carolina then gave the money back to Standard to pay off the Aunt Tilly's loan. Several other transactions of a similar nature were carried out by SLAC, in order to bail out unprofitable ventures and to make the parent look good.

INSUFFICIENT WORKING CAPITAL

Auditors should be especially concerned when a firm they are auditing experiences a cash shortage, a negative cash flow, or a lack of sufficient working capital and/or credit to enable them to continue their normal business operation (Touche Ross, 1974; Coopers & Lybrand, 1977; Arens and Loebbecke, 1976; Carmichael, 1975, and SAS 6, AICPA, 1975). In some cases, a cash shortage may occur at the same time the company is experiencing unusually high profits.

In the Penn Central case, the Pennsylvania Railroad merged with the New York Central Railroad in 1968. At a time when money was desperately needed to cope with the high start-up costs and other operational and financial problems caused by the merger, Penn Central invested $200 million into a diversification program. Management failed to make badly needed maintenance and repair of roads and equipment in order to further fund their diversification program. Most of the diversification investments were in real estate, which demanded large amounts of cash and left the company short of working capital. This problem was temporarily resolved by borrowing Eurodollars and Swiss francs at high interest rates and by issuing an enormous amount of commercial paper. Substantially all of Penn Central's investments and properties were placed as securities for these loans. Their cash position was further hurt by the regular payment of large dividends, high executive salaries, and difficulties in collecting receivables. All these factors made it difficult for Penn Central to meet its current obligations, and made the fraudulent misrepresentation they resorted to an attractive "solution" to their problems.

The lack of sufficient working capital was also a prime motivation for Equity Funding to initially create fictitious policies. At first, the creation and selling of fictitious policies was only a temporary solution. However, having to make payments on fraudulent policies sold to other insurance companies only made matters worse by further compounding their working capital problems in succeeding years. The effect of the scheme was a geometric growth of cash needs. As premiums became due, Equity Funding had to create and sell additional fictitious policies, which in turn created even greater cash needs in subsequent years. It was mathematical suicide.

HIGH DEBT

Excessive indebtedness or a need for even greater indebtedness to meet company obligations can place significant financial strains on a company (Coopers & Lybrand, 1977 and Kapnick, 1976). For example, the level of debt appeared to be far too high in the Ampex case. Ampex Corporation was a manufacturer of magnetic tapes and recording equipment that was started in 1946. In 1962, they had $14.7 million in debt and in 1971, their debt totaled $195.1 million. In the six years prior to litigation, this debt increased three times more than their sales increased. Because of their poor financial condition in 1971, Ampex filed an SEC report that was alleged to contain material misrepresentation that led to several law suits by stockholders.

Penn Central borrowed heavily, not only from banks, but also from the federal government. They also issued enormous amounts of commercial paper. Because of their constant need for cash and their high indebtedness, they had a practice of continually rolling over the commercial paper when it became due. This indebtedness was created, in part, by their payment of large dividends and their diversification into real estate.

Another example of a high debt red flag and several other red flags is the Omega-Alpha case (WSJ, 1975c). In 1975, the Securities and Exchange Commission (SEC) filed a complaint in federal district court charging Omega-Alpha with fraud in the sale of unregistered securities of the North American Acceptance Corp. The SEC claimed that North American financed its operation through the sale of promissory notes. They used the proceeds from the sale of additional notes to pay a substantial portion of the cost of notes that were maturing. Unfortunately, the company couldn't meet a sudden surge in demand for payments in February of 1974 that was triggered by a financial statement mailed to noteholders containing a disclaimer by its independent auditors. North American collapsed and the SEC alleged that they had made false and misleading statements and had omitted material facts in the sale of the notes. The alleged false and misleading statements were related to North American's negative cash flow, liquidity problems, losses, and the millions of dollars transferred from North American to Omega-Alpha for working capital and for the retirement of debt unrelated to North American.

REDUCED ABILITY TO ACQUIRE CREDIT

According to Coopers & Lybrand (1977), and SAS 6, AICPA, (1975), companies with a shortage of funds have a reduced ability to acquire credit and should be carefully scrutinized by their auditors. If a company is unable to raise money from the outside (through borrowing or equity financing) and is forced to generate funds internally through current earnings, it might be tempted to "manufacture" money through fraudulent transactions.

Tight credit appears to be at least part of the problem behind the collapse of Black Watch Farms, at one time the big-

gest cattle breeding company of its kind in the United States
with over 30,000 head of cattle in more than 20 states (WSJ,
1973a). However, court papers allege that prior to the collapse, approximately $3.2 million were misappropriated and
vital information about Black Watch Farms' poor financial condition was withheld from investors. The people that ran Black
Watch Farms blamed its collapse on a variety of causes, including tight credit, changes in the tax laws, and severe cash flow
problems.

PROFIT SQUEEZE

Coopers & Lybrand (1977) and Lane (1953) stated that a
likely candidate for fraud is a company with a profit squeeze
caused by sales and revenues not keeping pace with increasing
costs and expenses. In today's environment, where inflationary
and recessionary forces are so prevalent, this red flag becomes
especially important. As an example, the management of
Ampex was unable to control costs which increased twice as
much as sales over a period of several years.

RESTRICTIVE LOAN AGREEMENTS

An existing loan agreement with little flexibility and tough
restrictions is another red flag. Little available tolerance on
debt restrictions, such as maintenance of working capital and
limits on additional permissable debt, can place significant financial restrictions on companies (Touche Ross, 1974; and
Coopers & Lybrand, 1977).

An example of problems with debt obligations is the Fisco
Case (WSJ, 1974a). A Fisco shareholder filed a class action suite
charging Fisco with issuing misleading financial information in
1973. Fisco, in turn, sued its auditors for failing to conduct a
proper audit of its financial statements for 1972 and for failing
to uncover deficiencies in accounting procedures, data processing, and embezzlement by certain employees. The independent auditors had voiced concerns about Fisco's 1973
results. These concerns included the existence of defaults on
debt obligations that Fisco was trying to renegotiate, the possibility of a negative net worth, and the chance of significant
losses and cash flow problems in 1974.

PROGRESSIVE DETERIORATION IN QUALITY
OF CORPORATE EARNINGS

Coopers & Lybrand (1977) state that a "progressive deterioration in the 'quality' of earnings (e.g., the adoption of straight-line depreciation to replace sum-of-the-year's-digits depreciation without good reason) is a company pressure that should concern auditors." As previously mentioned, a deterioration of the earnings figures, especially over a period of years, can result in internal pressures on management and can also lead them to commit dishonest acts.

Beverly Hills Bancorp is an example of a company who got into trouble with the SEC due, in part, to deteriorating earnings. On August 13, 1974, the Securities and Exchange Commission filed a complaint in the federal district court of Los Angeles charging Beverly Hills Bancorp, a subsidiary, three officers, and an accounting firm with violating registration, antifraud, and reporting provisions of federal securities laws. Most of the defendants were also charged with filing false and misleading statements with the SEC, and with hiding the steadily deteriorating financial position of Beverly Hills Bancorp.

In its complaint, the SEC alleged that since the end of 1971, the defendants had engaged in a complex fraudulent scheme to raise money through tax-sheltered real estate projects in which the company provided loans to developers on the one hand, while raising money from public investors on the other. One of these loans was to Urbanetics for $7.6 million. When the real estate market began to collapse and the developers incurred substantial cost overruns, the company had to advance more money to cover itself. According to the SEC, the nature of these added loans was concealed from the public and the stockholders. Beverly Hills Bancorp was unable to retire immediate short-term commercial paper obligations because of delays in loan payments by Urbanetics, and finally filed a petition for reorganization under Chapter X of the federal bankruptcy act. The case never went to court, and one company official consented to a permanent injunction against any future violations of federal securities laws. Control of the company passed on to a court-appointed trustee who supervised a distribution of $12.2 million through a court-imposed liquidation plan.

URGENT NEED FOR FAVORABLE EARNINGS

Often the progress and evaluation of a firm, and especially of its management, is governed largely by the corporate earnings record. Because of the importance of earnings, it is easy to see why the urgent desire for a continued favorable earnings record, often in the hope of supporting the price of a company's stock, is the company red flag most often cited in the literature. (See, for example, Arens and Loebbecke, 1976; Carmichael, 1975; Coopers & Lybrand, 1977; Gottheimer, 1978; Foster, 1975; Kapnick, 1975; Touche Ross, 1974; and SAS 6, AICPA, 1975.)

In the trustee's report filed in accordance with Equity Funding's Chapter X bankruptcy proceedings, it stated that Equity Funding was a securities fraud and not an insurance fraud. Robertson (1973) suggests that Equity's president was concerned only with boosting the price of the company's stock, which he felt would come only through continued higher earnings. Woolf (1977) stated that with Equity's shares being publicly traded, its earnings became a matter of intense concern, especially among the salesmen and executives. He also stated that for the inner circle of senior officers with vast holdings of stock, increases in earnings were even more vital. In the Penn Central case, top management was alleged to have frequently sacrificed sound business practices to create the appearance of favorable financial results.

Two recent examples of alleged fraud involving manipulating earnings to support a high stock price are: U. S. Financial Inc., and Mattel, Inc. According to the SEC suit, U. S. Financial attempted to manipulate the price of its common stock to protect a director's net worth, which consisted mainly of shares of the company stock. The manipulation consisted of a scheme to create artificial revenues and profits in that company. Apparently, some of the director's stock was pledged as collateral on loans and a drop in stock price would seriously affect his borrowing power (WSJ, 1974). Revenues and earnings supposedly were fabricated by engaging in purported sales of real properties and other assets at substantial profit to U. S. Financial.

With Mattel, Inc., the SEC alleged that officials had a policy of maintaining the appearance of corporate growth, even though actual results didn't reflect those increases. The purpose of this "appearance of growth" was to "influence the market price of Mattel stock" and to borrow money from banks. As an example, a May 7, 1970 memo reports that senior management officials set target results of a 22 percent sales increase and per-share earnings of 19 cents for the first quarter that had ended five days earlier. The targets were to be used to manipulate actual figures, according to that report. The memo is an example of setting "arbitrary requirements" for sales and earnings to create the appearance that such sales and earnings were steadily increasing; this would, in turn, influence the price of Mattel stock (WSJ, 1973, 1978).

NEED TO GLOSS OVER A TEMPORARILY BAD SITUATION

Kapnick (1976) stated that one possible incentive for committing fraud is an attempt to gloss over what is believed to be a temporarily bad situation, in order to retain management control or prestige. He states that the incentive for gain need not necessarily be an immediate, direct, or even an indirect monetary gain. The hoped-for gain might be sometime in the future, or even a preservation of the current remuneration received by corporate employees. Richard Marx, a criminal lawyer, said that fraud perpetrators, when business gets a little bad, rationalize activities as necessary in order to save their businesses (Blustein, 1978).

Republic National Life had been a strong and respected insurance company for over 35 years. However, they made some losing investments in a subsidiary: Realty Equity Corporation. In an attempt to salvage these investments, Republic invested a substantial amount of additional money into Realty. In 1974, the SEC filed a suit citing Republic, Realty, their respective auditors, and 11 key individuals for (1) investing substantial amounts of money in an attempt to protect and conceal their failing investments in Realty; (2) concealing these further investments from Republic's stockholders and the Texas Insurance Commission by channelling the investments through third parties; (3) fraudulently diverting income of Republic to Realty, who returned the funds as interest income, and (4) grossly overstating the assets by using poor accounting principles, such as the most favorable method of land valuation.

Another example is the Penn Central case. Its former top officials were accused of directing a massive fraud scheme prior to the 1970 bankruptcy filing of its railroad subsidiary. The alleged reasons for extensive financial mismanagement and deceit were to give the impression that Penn Central was a sound company. Despite the absence of cash earnings, Penn Central continued to pay dividends annually in order to conceal from investors and creditors the critical condition of the company. The complaint also charged Penn Central with making false statements about its borrowings. These actions were evidently made in hopes of forestalling a financial crisis long enough to allow the company to work out its financial problems.

UNMARKETABLE COLLATERAL

Coopers & Lybrand (1977) stated that the existence of unmarketable collateral can motivate management to commit fraud. This was the situation with the Continental Vending case, in which the $2.9 million collateral in stock pledged on loans dropped over $2 million in value.

DEPENDENCE ON ONE OR TWO PRODUCTS, CUSTOMERS, OR TRANSACTIONS

A company dependent upon only one or relatively few products, customers, or transactions is in a very vulnerable position when one of them is lost. If the financial well-being of the company is in question, managers might resort to fraud as a solution (Coopers & Lybrand, 1977; Touche Ross, 1974; Carmichael, 1975; Arens and Loebbecke, 1976; and SAS 6, AICPA, 1975). An example is Sterling Homex, which depended upon the government to purchase their housing units. When a major government contract did not materialize, they resorted to the fraudulent reporting of unearned revenues.

EXCESS CAPACITY

Economic or other conditions (such as energy shortages) can result in a company having idle productive capacity, thereby depriving a company of its normal means of generating income. As a company's income decreases, it becomes increasingly more susceptible to criticism and pressures from stockholders, creditors, and others (Touche Ross & Co., 1974; Coopers & Lybrand, 1977; and Arens and Loebbecke, 1976, and SAS 6, AICPA, 1975). Fraud is viewed by some managers as a means of alleviating the criticism and pressures.

SEVERE OBSOLESCENCE

Some firms operate in industries where technological advancements or developments can quickly make products obsolete (Coopers & Lybrand, 1977; and Arens and Loebbecke, 1976; and SAS 6, AICPA, 1975). Penn Central, for example, apparently was still carrying on its books a number of box cars that were located in old abandoned mines, along with other inventory that was of no practical value to the company. The inventory at Ampex increased over 185 percent in six years without a comparable increase in sales. In addition, an SEC investigation revealed that Ampex failed to write off assets that were obsolete and worthless.

LONG BUSINESS CYCLE

Coopers & Lybrand (1977) and Touche Ross (1974) stated that a long manufacturing cycle may have an adverse economic impact when costs are rising and products have been sold at fixed prices or in competitive markets. These adverse conditions are situational pressures that make fraud more likely than normal. Inflationary pressures can contribute to the impact of a long business cycle, thereby increasing a firm's motivation to engage in fraud.

EXISTENCE OF REVOCABLE AND POSSIBLY IMPERILED LICENSES

Both Touche Ross (1974) and Coopers & Lybrand (1977) claimed that the existence of revocable and possibly imperiled licenses necessary for the continuation of the business can pose a threat that might give rise to fraudulent acts. In the Republic National Life case, Republic's licenses were in jeopardy when the Texas State Insurance Commissioner ordered that a state of supervision be placed on Republic. This was also a significant factor in the collapse of Black Watch Farms. (See: Significant Tax Adjustments or Changes section in this chapter.) The threat of losing a license and not being able to continue operations represents intense situational pressures that contribute to the likelihood of fraud.

EXTREMELY RAPID EXPANSION

Firms experiencing rapid expansion of new business or product lines resulting in massive demands for new capital should be evaluated closely (Touche Ross, 1974; Coopers & Lybrand, 1977; and Carmichael, 1975). In the Salad Oil case, The Allied Crude Vegetable Oil Refining Corporation was started with $500,000 capital. Within a very short time, the company was the supplier of 85 percent of the salad oil for government's Food for Peace program that sold surplus crops to foreign countries. When the fraud was finally uncovered, Allied Crude Vegetable claimed to have more salad oil than existed in all the United States, and the eventual losses were modestly placed at $200 million spread over some 51 major banking and brokerage concerns in the U.S. and Europe. Another example is the Westec case, which was transformed from a small company with annual net earnings of $270,000 to a 17-company conglomerate with earnings of over $5 million in approximately 18 months.

UNFAVORABLE ECONOMIC CONDITIONS WITHIN AN INDUSTRY

A firm operating in a situation where the industry is declining or is characterized by a large number of business failures is more susceptable to fraudulent practices than one operating in a growing and robust economic environment (Carmichael, 1975; Coopers & Lybrand, 1977; and SAS 6, AICPA, 1975). This red flag becomes especially meaningful when a firm's stated performance is contrary to industry trends.

As an example, Equity Funding appeared to make a dramatic comeback in the latter part of 1970 and 1971, when the insurance industry was suffering severe economic decline. New sales were down for the industry, and existing policy holders were not renewing their insurance. Stock prices for Equity Funding, which had been $80 per share only one year before, were at $12 per share toward the end of 1970. In late 1970, Equity Funding began reinsuring fictitious policies. Sales skyrocketed and the reported insurance tripled in force. The industry was amazed at Equity Funding's ability to turn its program around and show surprising gains while everyone else was experiencing a severe economic decline.

In the Salad Oil case, the Allied Crude Vegetable Oil Refining Corp. was in a fiercely competitive business. Nevertheless, it bought new and modern equipment and buildings, paid the highest wages, bought oil at high prices, and then underbid all the competition for government contracts. No one could fathom how Allied made money out of those deals. Allied's efforts to corner the market by dealing in future commodities occurred in a period when official export market reports were the most pessimistic in years. Yet their buying continued in a magnitude greater than the commodity exchanges had ever experienced.

In 1975, eight ex-officials of the collapsed Franklin National Bank (WSJ, 1975a) were charged by a grand jury with misapplying more than $30 million of the bank's funds. The men sold, for future delivery, more foreign currencies than it purchased, resulting in an enormous and unauthorized "short position," with a dollar value exceeding $400 million. The grand jury charged that the men intended to maintain this short position, hoping that the value of the foreign currencies would decline, so that the bank could then purchase foreign currencies for substantially less than the sale price of the future contracts, thus making a substantial profit. When the foreign currencies did not decline, the eight men tried to cover up substantial losses by making false entries in the books, resulting in the bank issuing false statements.

An attempt to cover up substantial losses threatening to significantly impair the ability of Weis Securities, Inc. to remain solvent resulted in a grand jury indictment of five top officers of the collapsed security firm (WSJ, 1973b). The federal grand jury charged the men with falsifying books and records to show a $1.7 million profit for the year ended May 1972, when the firm actually had losses of more than $1.5 million.

DIFFICULTY IN COLLECTING RECEIVABLES

A company can experience financial stress when it has difficulty collecting accounts receivable from customers. This is especially important when the company's customers are experiencing severe economic pressures (Touche Ross, 1974 and Coopers & Lybrand, 1977). Penn Central, for example, had $51.6 million in uncollectable receivables in May 1968. By May 1970, these receivables had skyrocketed to over $100.5 million. Continental Vending's inability to collect a $3.5 million loan from its affiliate, Valley Commercial Corporation, led to the SEC suspending trade of Continental Vending's stock on the American Stock Exchange.

Another example of problems stemming from uncollectable receivables was one experienced by Co-Build Corporation, where over $2 million in receivables were in default and sales of a nonrecurring nature, to employees and/or persons related to Co-Build, created receivables of "doubtful collectability." Giant Stores, likewise had approximately $300,000 of advertising credits that had not been collected (WSJ, 1973c, 1979b).

UNUSUALLY HEAVY COMPETITION

Companies in industries experiencing unusually heavy competition (developing industries, competition with low-priced imports, etc.) often find themselves unable to show favorable net income and earnings per share figures (Touche Ross, 1974 and Coopers & Lybrand, 1977).

SIGNIFICANT REDUCTION IN SALES BACKLOGS, INDICATING FUTURE SALES DECLINE

Coopers & Lybrand (1977) felt that a firm experiencing a significant reduction in sales backlogs that indicates a decline in future sales, would have a greater incentive for becoming involved in fraudulent practices than firms facing no such stress.

PRESSURE TO MERGE

Both Touche Ross (1974) and Coopers & Lybrand (1977) stated that many acquisitions of speculative ventures in an attempt to diversify should be of special concern to auditors. Jaspan (1972) mentioned that corporate mergers often have marked impact on dishonesty. Instead of making a contribution, a merger can drain corporate profits. Mergers and acquisitions entered into in order to increase sales and profits, may, in fact, foster disloyalty and frustration due to insecurity and unfulfilled expectations. These feelings are reinforced when conglomerates and other companies accelerate their liquidation of marginal operations during a recession. Klein and Densmore (1977) also claimed that a merger can be one of the most significant motivators for fraud because uncertainty about the future may dissolve employee loyalty. Knowing that the odds against prosecution are high, they may steal to fill the void created by insecurity.

In the Tally case, the plaintiffs charged that there were two main parts to Tally's scheme to acquire General Time Corporation. The first involved the manipulation of General Time's stock prices downward, and the concurrent manipulation of Tally's stock prices upward. Thus, General Time's stockholders would receive less than fair value at the time of the merger when their stock was exchanged for Tally stock. This manipulation allegedly began shortly after the election of a Tally slate of officers to the General Time board of directors and continued until the time of the merger.

In the Georgia Pacific case, the SEC charged that corporate officers practiced fraud and deceit by manipulating the price of company stock through transactions made for the employees' stock bonus trust. The St. Croix Paper Company filed suit for $10 million in damages, alleging that Georgia Pacific had, through stock manipulations using the employees' stock bonus trust funds, defrauded its stockholders of 118,000 shares of stock when the two companies merged.

SIZABLE INVENTORY INCREASE WITHOUT
COMPARABLE SALES INCREASE

Coopers & Lybrand (1977) suggested that a company finding itself with a sizable *inventory* increase without a comparable *sales* increase, could be a likely candidate for illegal actions. This situation might be indicative of a company's inability to maintain its market share. This inability, plus the fact that production is not scaled down, results in an inventory glut. The resulting cash shortage might motivate a company to turn to fraudulent means to restore vitality to its organization.

SIGNIFICANT TAX ADJUSTMENTS OR CHANGES

Coopers & Lybrand (1977) indicated that significant tax adjustments by the IRS are especially important when they occur with some regularity. Regular tax adjustments might indicate that a company is manipulating its earnings figures. The Continental Vending case is an illustration of a firm having significant tax adjustments prior to the fraudulent activities.

A significant tax change that discouraged investors from buying cattle was one of the major contributors to the collapse of Black Watch Farms Inc. (WSJ, 1973a). Black Watch managed over 30,000 head of cattle in 20 states. The 570 herd owners, which included many highly-paid business, professional, and entertainment people, invested in cattle to gain tax write-offs and in the hope of making fat profits by selling the offspring of their cattle. However, changes in the tax laws eliminated the tax write-offs and began discouraging investors from buying cattle. In addition, the SEC ruled that the investment contracts by which the animals were sold were a security and thus had to be registered with the commission. When the SEC later refused to clear Black Watch's prospectus, it meant that the farm couldn't sell any more cattle. Black Watch began to experience difficulties because cash flow was down and the only dependable source of cash was new investors. Black Watch then issued a press release indicating that, in the judgment of the management, Black Watch had reached an optimum size for economic operations and would not be selling any additional breeding herds. As a result, papers were filed in New York District Court, alleging that Black Watch had withheld vital information about its poor financial shape from investors. The papers also alleged that several officers of the company misappropriated $3.2 million of company funds.

SIGNIFICANT LITIGATION

Touche Ross (1974), Coopers & Lybrand (1977), Foster (1975), and SAS 6, AICPA, (1975) indicated that the existence of significant litigation, especially between stockholders and management, should be of concern to auditors. In the Homestake Production case, for example, stockholder litigation occurred in 1966, 1968, 1971, and 1972. In 1971, the SEC obtained an injunction against Homestake for "violation of anti-fraud and regulation provisions." In the Salad Oil case, the president was indicted many times by regulatory agencies for fraudulent practices.

SUSPENSION OR DELISTING FROM A STOCK EXCHANGE

Several companies involved in fraudulent activities had been suspended or delisted from a stock exchange. In most instances, however, by the time the delisting or suspension took place, the fraudulent practices were public knowledge and would not have served as predictive red flags (e.g., the Equity Funding and Continental Vending cases). One example where it could have served as a red flag, however, is the Allied Crude Vegetable case. The Adolph Gobal Co. was delisted because it understated losses in its stockholders reports. In addition, the Chicago Board of Trade and the Commodity Exchange Authority investigated Allied and found that Allied had illegally traded with itself to avoid taking delivery of future orders.

VALIDATION OF COMPANY PRESSURE RED FLAGS

In this chapter, we have reviewed 25 factors that suggest management may have an incentive to commit fraud on behalf of a company. In Table 1 of Appendix D, the results of a validation of these red flags, against 52 past cases of fraud, are presented. As the table shows, several of these 25 factors were evident in many of the cases.

* SUMMARY POINTS OF CHAPTER 3 *

* Company financial pressures that can lead to fraud are:
    1) heavy investments or losses
    2) insufficient working capital
    3) unusually high debt
    4) reduced ability to acquire credit
    5) profit squeeze
    6) restrictive loan agreements
    7) progressive deterioration in quality of earnings
    8) urgent need for favorable earnings
    9) need to gloss over temporarily bad situations
    10) unmarketable collateral.
* Company limitations that can lead to fraud are:
    1) dependence upon only one or two products
    2) dependence upon only one or two customers
    3) excess capacity
    4) severe obsolescence
    5) extremely long business cycle
    6) existence of revokable or imperiled licenses.
* Business decisions that can lead to fraud are:
    1) extremely rapid expansion
    2) publishing of overly optimistic earnings forecasts.
* External economic conditions that can lead to fraud are:
    1) unfavorable economic conditions within an industry
    2) difficulty in collecting receivables
    3) unusually heavy competition
    4) significant reduction in sales backlog
    5) pressure to merge
    6) sizeable inventory increase without a comparable sales increase.
* Legal difficulties that can lead to fraud are:
    1) significant tax adjustments
    2) significant litigation, especially between stockholders and management
    3) suspension or delisting from a stock exchange.

4

OPPORTUNITIES
THAT
ALLOW OR
ENCOURAGE
MANAGEMENT
FRAUD

Chapter 4 Explains:

- Relationships with outside parties that make fraud easier to commit.
- Organizational structures that make fraud easier to commit.
- Economic environments that make fraud easier to commit.
- Accounting practices that make fraud easier to commit.

Opportunities refer to situations where fraud is easier to commit, where the detection is not as likely, or where the probability of prosecution is low. Anything that creates more convenient opportunities increases the probability of fraud. To detect fraud, auditors need to look for convenient opportunities. The fact that convenient opportunities exist does not mean that a fraud will necessarily occur, but when these factors exist, the probability of fraud is higher, signaling that auditors should look more closely for improper actions. The major opportunities can be grouped into four categories: (a) opportunities that are created by relationships with outside parties, (b) opportunities created by complex organizational structures, (c) opportunities created by economic environments, and (d) opportunities created by inadequate accounting practices.

This chapter examines the corporate structures and practices that create opportunities for key individuals in a company to commit fraud for corporate benefit. The 17 specific red flags considered are:

1. Related-Party transactions
2. The use of several different auditing firms, or the frequent changing of auditors
3. Reluctance to give auditors needed data
4. The use of several different legal firms or the frequent changing of legal counsels
5. The use of an unusually large number of banks, none of which can see the entire picture
6. Continuous problems with various regulatory agencies
7. A complex business structure
8. No effective internal auditing staff
9. High degree of computerization in the firm
10. Inadequate internal control system, or failure to enforce existing internal controls
11. Rapid turnover of key employees
12. Involvement in atypical or "hot" industries
13. Large year-end and/or unusual transactions
14. Unduly liberal accounting practices
15. Poor accounting records
16. Inadequately staffed accounting department
17. Inadequate disclosure of questionable or unusual accounting practices.

RELATED-PARTY TRANSACTIONS

Related-Party transactions are transactions resulting from corporate officers dealing among themselves, with affiliated companies, with family members, or with shell companies. These business transactions are characterized by their non-independence. Some common examples are borrowing or lending funds with interest rates below the current market, selling assets at prices significantly different from appraised values, and exchanging property and making loans with no repayment schedule.

Arens and Loebbecke (1976) and Kapnick (1976) both mentioned the last factor above as a possible indicator of fraud. The American Institute of Public Accountants published a Statement on Auditing Standards devoted entirely to this issue (SAS 6, AICPA, 1975). Foster (1975) indicated that a clue to the occurrence of fraud is a situation in which management is indebted to the company and the amount is large enough to question whether it will be repaid.

There are many cases in which related-party transactions were a salient factor in the frauds. Continental Vending had several related-party transactions with its affiliate, Valley Commercial Corporation, and its president. Another example is the Co-Build Corporation case, a Virgin Island company accused of overstating sales during the years 1969-1972. One of the factors alleged in the suit was that Co-Build had several transactions with a prime contractor which were not adequately disclosed in the financial statements. Supposedly, inventory and other transactions between the two parties had a significant effect on the cost of goods sold and on profits (WSJ, 1973c).

SEVERAL DIFFERENT AUDITING FIRMS

Touche Ross (1974) suggested that a company that uses different auditors for the various major segments of their business is more susceptible to fraud. Touche Ross seemed to imply that one possible motivation for a firm having several auditors is so that no one auditor can see the complete picture or trace a major transaction from beginning to end. Certainly this factor was present in Equity Funding, where different auditors were retained for most of the major subsidiaries.

Foster (1975) indicated that a firm having a past history of switching auditors is more likely to be involved in fraudulent activities than one that has not done so. This seems logical, since a firm that suspects its auditors are getting close to detection would fire the auditors. Also, a CPA firm that concluded or even had a hunch that management was not trustworthy, or was involved in illegal activities, would probably resign. Another reason the frequent changing of auditors creates increased suspicions of or opportunities for fraud is because new auditors do not know as much about the firm as those who have been auditing it for several years. The ignorance of a new auditor tends to reduce both the likelihood and the fear that fraud will be discovered. The National Student Marketing, the Homestake Production, the Sterling Homex, and the Republican National Life cases all occurred in the first or second year in which a new auditor had accepted those firms as clients.

After reviewing the actual fraud cases, two members of our research team felt so strongly about this red flag that they wrote a separate paper (Romney and Albrecht, 1979) encouraging auditors to closely scrutinize any potential new client. Auditing firms should be aware that, when they accept a new client, the probability of fraudulent activity is much greater than with an existing client. When investigating potential clients, both the principals and the company itself should be examined. While each circumstance will differ and professional judgment must be exercised, an investigation of the principals should include the following seven items.

1. *Underworld or questionable connections.* In a number of cases on the public record, executives were accused of having connections with either the underworld or other questionable associates. Detective agencies have found that criminal infiltration is especially likely when an organization's structure is composed of many obscure, small companies that are frequently represented by the same attorney.

2. *Financial history.* A thorough check should be conducted to determine credit history, heavy indebtedness, previous bankruptcies, and whether principals are living beyond their means. In our review of over 100 fraud cases, there were very few instances where embezzlers hoarded their illegally obtained funds. Almost without exception, they enjoyed life-styles that were significantly beyond their reported incomes.

3. *Employment history.* Investigations of past employment histories, in certain cases, should include: examinations of the number of years worked with the company; previous employers or involvement with other business; attitudes; reputation among associates;

and reasons for terminating previous affiliations. For example, in checking on the controller of a prospective client, one CPA firm found that he had been fired from three of five previous jobs in the last eight years, one of which involved an embezzlement. At his last job as a controller, he was discharged when an executive of the parent company appeared on an unannounced nocturnal inspection and found a complete stranger working on the corporate books. This outsider proved to be the secret employee of the controller and was performing his accounting functions at night.

4. *Undesirable conduct.* Investigations in this area may necessitate a review of certain of the principal's habits (such as gambling, drug abuse, or other intemperate habits that might compromise the client's reputation). If the need arises, places frequented and contacts with friends and business associates may need to be investigated. In one investigation of which we are aware, the CPA firm did not accept a potential client after finding that one of the important principals had excessive gambling debts. Later, that principal, his company, and the CPA firm subsequently accepting the company as a client, were all victims of substantial fraud litigation.

5. *Past criminal background.* A thorough check of court records, newspaper logs, and other litigation records will reveal any past litigation in which key executives have been involved.

6. *Personal reputations and demographics.* In this area, items such as personal integrity, attitude, and educational background should be examined. In many cases, principals have lied about their backgrounds. For example, an executive obtained his initial loan to buy a drug company by lying to a banker. He claimed to have a doctorate degree in medicine from the University of Heidelberg. He gave the impression that his medical background would enable him to effectively manage the drug operation.

7. *Conflicts of interest.* Ownership interest by executives

in competitive companies, major suppliers, or major customers may be a problem and may be revealed during an investigation of a client's principal officers.

In investigating the corporation, many of these same factors, such as past litigation, economic history, and corporate reputation should be examined. As with the investigations of the executives, these corporate factors would also be investigated by examining legal records, newspaper logs, credit checks, attorneys, banks, investment bankers, and even governmental agencies. In addition, however, the auditor should be keenly aware of certain other factors. When an auditor's preliminary evaluation of the following items yields unsatisfactory results, an investigative agency should be used to examine them more closely.

1. *Consumer and vendor history.* A key factor in many of the documented frauds has been excessively close relationships with key consumers and vendors. For example, Stirling Homex had questionable or illegitimate business relationships with nearly all of the buyers of its land deals.

2. *Personnel policies and practices.* Where required, investigative action should be conducted regarding the turnover and the background of key employees. High turnover is indicative of internal problems, many of which could be caused by illegal or unethical practices.

3. *Organizational structure.* Two important areas of organizational structure need to be examined: the organization of the company itself and the company's relationships with outside parties, such as bankers, attorneys, and CPA firms. Investigations should be conducted to determine the sources of financial backing, the complexities of the organizational structure and the purposes and the nature of subsidiaries and other related corporations. When considering relationships with outside parties, the number and nature of relationships should be investigated. A common characteristic of past fraud cases is the retaining of several banks, lawyers, or CPA firms, none of which had a full picture of their client's total operations. For example,

Tino De Angelis, mastermind of the great Salad Oil Scandal, borrowed from several different banks and investment houses, none of which knew the extent of the other loaners' interests. Auditors and investigative agencies should also be prepared to closely examine any situation in which only one individual with long tenure has control of a company's money, especially when the executives above this person are relatively new to the organization.

RELUCTANCE TO GIVE AUDITORS NEEDED DATA

Coopers and Lybrand (1977) suggested that a reluctance by management to provide additional information to improve the clarity and comprehensiveness of the company's financial statements is a potential indicator of fraud. In addition, we were personally told by representatives of several auditing firms, as well as by SEC personnel, that the occurrence of many unplanned surprises for auditors can signal the existence of fraud. In particular, they said that if an auditor is constantly faced with unplanned surprises, he should question whether or not they are legitimate.

SEVERAL DIFFERENT LEGAL COUNSELS

Touche Ross (1974) indicated that the company that has no outside general counsel, but instead uses special counsel for individual matters, or a firm using outside general counsel that seems to switch with some frequency, is a likely candidate for fraud. If a firm has no outside general counsel who knows all of the legal ramifications of the firm's business, it is much easier to carry on fraudulent activities. Certainly, any company that uses several different outside legal counsels, or one that switches outside counsel with some frequency, should be viewed cautiously. This factor was evident in National Student Marketing, where their legal counsel resigned just prior to the revelation of improper activities. An SEC commissioner indicated that switching counsels may be an alternative to providing damaging information to existing legal counsel.

THE USE OF AN UNUSUALLY LARGE NUMBER OF BANKS

A firm that uses an unusually large number of banks may be trying to hide something. This is especially true if the banks are being used as sources of funding. For example, in the Salad Oil Case, De Angelis used an extremely large number of banks for funding, pledging the same collateral on many loans. The failure of that company alone had a ripple effect, which caused the bankruptcy of approximately 20 banks.

CONTINUOUS PROBLEMS WITH REGULATORY AGENCIES

A continuous problem with regulatory agencies was first mentioned by Sutherland (1956). He selected seventy large industrial and commercial corporations in the United States and investigated the number and nature of their adverse regulatory decisions. He found that every one of the 70 corporations had a regulatory agency decision against them, and that there were a total of 980 adverse decisions, or an average of 14 per firm. Of the corporations studied, 98 percent had two or more adverse decisions against them. Using a figure of four convictions, a number that defines a habitual criminal in several states, he concluded that 90 percent of the corporations in his sample were comparable to habitual criminals. As examples, Homestake Oil, Stirling Homex, Republic National Life, National Student Marketing, and Penn Central all experienced early problems with various regulatory agencies, including the SEC.

COMPLEX BUSINESS STRUCTURE

Kapnick (1975) and Touche Ross (1974) listed an artificially complex business structure as another clue of possible fraud. One of the most effective ways to commit fraud is to establish a complex corporate structure having different auditors, bankers, and legal counsels for the different parts of the corporation, thereby not allowing any one party access to all the pieces or parts of any particular transaction. This was the case with Equity Funding. Although the corporate structure was not overly complex, there were a number of very complex transactions between subsidiaries. In addition, it was the complex business structure of utility firms and the implicit danger of such structures that led the SEC to pass the Public Utility Holding Company Act of 1935. At that time, the SEC saw a system of huge utility empires controlling widely scattered subsidiaries that had no functional relationship to each other. The companies were put into a pyramid together, layer upon layer, and possessed complex capital structures that were confusing to investors, with a high potential for fraud.

LACK OF AN EFFECTIVE INTERNAL AUDITING STAFF

Touche Ross (1974), Kapnick (1975) and Foster (1975) included as a red flag the company that seems to need, but lacks, an internal auditing staff. Psychological theory would suggest that where there is an organization (such as an internal auditing staff) that provides some deterrent or fear of being caught, the opportunity to commit crime is decreased. In most of the fraud cases we studied, an effective internal auditing staff was absent.

A HIGHLY-COMPUTERIZED FIRM

Foster (1975), in listing several factors that were associated with recent frauds, included a "highly-computerized business." He indicated that such businesses are susceptible to fraud because of the ease with which a skilled person can both defraud and reduce the probability of detection. Jaspan (1972) indicated that the vulnerability of a computer to fraud by dishonest employees is a major management concern. He says that some executives assume that automation and computers reduce the possibility of embezzlement because a machine, by its very nature, is immune to corruption and temptation. They forget that humans operate the equipment. If dishonest operators, programmers, or systems analysts distort programs or feed incorrect data into the system, the machines will process the information, accurate as well as inaccurate, without knowing the difference. In several of his writings, Donn Parker (SRI International) has indicated that because of the proliferation of the computer, future frauds will generally be larger than those of the past. Since, with the computer, audit trails have diminished and safeguards are not yet fully developed, it seems reasonable to assume that the computer would increase the opportunity for trained people to commit fraud. This is especially true since, at this time, there is no code of professional ethics for data processing personnel.

Two of the most highly-publicized cases where computers were heavily involved in fraud were those of Equity Funding (Loeffler) and Jimmy S., the person who defrauded the Pacific Telephone Company of approximately $1 million. In late 1978, there was the case of an individual in California who made a $9 million wire transfer from a California bank to a Swiss bank on a Radio Shack computer from the telephone in his apartment. He then used the proceeds to purchase Russian diamonds.

INADEQUATE INTERNAL CONTROL

The most common red flag is probably an inadequate system of, or the nonenforcement of, existing internal controls. Much of the compliance testing and internal control checks performed by CPAs in their audits stems from the belief that a poor internal control system increases the opportunities to commit fraud. The lack of internal control was mentioned as a red flag numerous times in the literature. In most instances, it was said that there must have been poor internal control any time management fraud takes place. Jaspan (1972) stated that after forty years of experience in helping management control losses, he has discovered several methods to destroy the roots of dishonesty. One of these is unpredictability in establishing and enforcing controls. He says that spot checks are especially effective when introducing an internal control system, and that the insertion of occasional deliberate errors into the system as a test of employee integrity is helpful. He suggests that, in every company, an attitude should exist in which employees feel that such a test can occur at any time, without warning, as a normal and accepted part of operations. Rauchlin (1977) added that the surest avenue to fraud prevention and detection is a proper system of internal control, conscientiously implemented by management and regularly reviewed by auditors.

The lack of internal controls has been cited by several embezzlers as justification for their illegal acts. Many believed they were completely honest, and some have even gone so far as to say such things as "My crime was your fault; you let me do it, you made it possible for me to steal," or, "You had loose internal controls." Companies should be especially careful to ensure that existing and functioning internal control systems are not overlooked for crash programs or other types of pet projects.

An example of a fraud committed in a setting of poor internal controls was the fraud committed against the Perini Corp. in 1971. Approximately $1,150,000 in checks were written on the company's accounts by an outsider. Access to the checks was easy, because Perini kept its supply of unused checks in the same unlocked storeroom where the styrofoam coffee cups were stored. Every clerk and secretary had access to the storeroom, and the checks had been written on a check-writing machine that automatically signed the president's name. Despite inherent control procedures in the machine and Arthur Anderson's warning to implement them, Perini had found it inconvenient to use most control procedures. For example: the machine dumped signed checks into a box that was supposed to be locked; the key was supposed to be kept by an employee from a different department. No such employee was assigned, however, and the box was kept unlocked. Nor did anyone pay attention to the machine's counter, which kept track of the number of checks written, so that the number of checks could be compared with the number of vouchers authorized for payment. These and other inadequacies in control made the theft quite easy to commit (WSJ, September 10, 1975b).

RAPID TURNOVER OF KEY EMPLOYEES

Another characteristic that fosters opportunities for fraud is the rapid turnover of key employees, either through firing or voluntary terminations. In cases where there is rapid turnover, inexperienced people are placed in positions that are sometimes beyond their capabilities. Also, key employees often quit because they do not agree with the dishonest attitudes of other key officials. Carmichael and Willingham (1975), and Arens and Loebbecke (1976) cited rapid turnover as a red flag; it is also one of the warning signals included in the Coopers & Lybrand (1977) and Touche Ross (1974) audit checklists.

As an example of rapid turnover, Equity Funding had several controllers who resigned within a short period of time. Michael P. suddenly quit in 1969, at which time George R. took his place. When George R. discovered the irregularities, he went to the president and refused to sign SEC documents concerning the financial condition of the company. The president offered George R. a promotion which he initially accepted but later declined. Shortly thereafter, he left Equity Funding and Douglas S. then took over as controller; he was eventually implicated in the fraud (Loeffler, 1974).

FIRMS IN ATYPICAL OR "HOT" INDUSTRIES

During a private interview, one of the commissioners of the SEC stated that many frauds occur in atypical or "hot" industries. As an example, he referred to the disproportionately high number of frauds occurring in the diamond, coal, silver, and real estate industries.

LARGE YEAR-END AND/OR UNUSUAL TRANSACTIONS

Foster (1975) and Kapnick (1975) indicated that a large, unusual, or complex transaction, particularly at year-end, is a possible fraud signal. They suggested that large year-end transactions are often fabricated to change the picture of what otherwise might be a bad financial year for a corporation. Touche Ross (1974) suggested that if an audit closing requires numerous substantive adjusting entries, auditors should be alerted to the possible existence of fraud. Large year-end transactions were prevalent in many of the cases we analyzed. As an example, two unusual year-end transactions that occurred in Four Seasons Nursing Home were the sale of a Falcon Fan Jet to the Company for $1.5 million, and the payment of a large finder's fee to outsiders in order to get securities placed with institutions (*Forbes*, 1970).

LIBERAL ACCOUNTING PRACTICES

Foster (1975) indicated that a common factor in many of the recent fraud cases is that they were all companies having

unduly liberal accounting practices, such as recognizing revenue before its collectability is assured, or delaying the recognition of expenses as long as possible. Often, such unduly liberal
accounting practices concern only one major accounting transaction in a firm. For example, a firm that has normal or conservative accounting practices in all other areas, but is
extremely liberal in recognizing income should be viewed cautiously. Many practicing CPAs insist that they can identify
which of their clients have liberal accounting practices. One
partner in the Philadelphia office of a major CPA firm confid-
ed that he has an excellent knowledge of which of his clients
push accounting principles to the limit.

An example of liberal accounting is the case of Firestone
Group Ltd., a California real estate company. In 1969, Firestone offered securities for sale. One month prior to the offering, Firestone purchased and resold certain nursing homes:
transactions involving several million dollars. In accounting for
the transactions, Firestone recognized $2 million in current
and deferred profits, even though it paid only $30,000 as a
cash down payment and received only $25,000 in cash from its
purchaser. Subsequently, the purchaser didn't meet a $5 mil-
lion payment due and Firestone didn't meet its own obligation
to pay $4 million. The transaction boosted Firestone's reported
sales to $22 million from $6.7 million and converted a
$169,000 loss to a $66,000 profit. Given the small cash payments, the recognition of large profits was certainly questionable (WSJ, 1974b).

POOR ACCOUNTING RECORDS

Arens and Loebbecke (1976) and Kapnick (1975) suggested that a firm that has poor accounting records is more
susceptible to fraud than one that does not. In reviewing the
trustees report of Equity Funding, EDPACS, the EDP Audit
Control and Security newsletter, said that Equity's books and
records were always a mess. If the auditors had insisted that
the company keep adequate records, the fraud would have
been much more difficult to perpetrate. Another example is
the Rhode Island Hospital Trust National Bank, where, in the
year of the fraud, the records were so poorly maintained that

financial statements were completed three months later than expected.

INADEQUATE STAFFING IN THE ACCOUNTING DEPARTMENT

Kapnick (1975), Touche Ross (1974), and Foster (1975) indicated that an inadequately supervised and staffed accounting department, which is always behind in its work and is continually fighting fires in a crisis atmosphere, is a signal for fraud. Holmes (1976), in reviewing the Roadships Limited case, suggested that "Roadships' accounting records were in poor shape and their accounting staff was inadequate." Certainly the accounting staff of National Student Marketing was inadequate. In that company, at the time of litigation, the accountants were over two months behind in posting journal entries.

INADEQUATE DISCLOSURE OF QUESTIONABLE OR UNUSUAL ACCOUNTING PRACTICES

The final opportunity created by poor accounting practices is an inadequate disclosure of questionable or unusual accounting procedures. While this factor was not explicitly mentioned in the literature, it was suggested to us by several CPA partners. These partners indicated that many of their clients who have accounting practices unique to their firm or industry are reluctant to adequately disclose these types of practices. For example, Ampex failed to disclose such things as contingent liabilities, royalty guarantees, the discontinuation of product lines, and the deferring of research and development costs.

VALIDATION OF COMPANY OPPORTUNITY RED FLAGS

There are many opportunity factors or red flags that contribute to creating an atmosphere where fraud is more likely to occur. In this chapter, opportunity factors that allow management to commit fraudulent activities on behalf of the firm were discussed.

This chapter has highlighted these red flags and referenced the sources where they have been mentioned. These red flags have also been examined in the context of approximately 52 past fraud cases. A summary of the results of this comparative analysis is presented in Table 2 of Appendix D. This table shows that all the red flags discussed can be associated with at least one major fraud. Some of the factors listed here do not seem like opportunities. However, each of the factors, either directly or indirectly, creates an increased opportunity for fraud; auditors and firms who monitor these red flags can use this information to detect and reduce its incidence. Finally, it should be remembered that the presence of one, or even all, of these factors does not necessarily guarantee the existence of fraud. We suggest, however, that fraud might be one concomitant of their occurrence and should be explicitly considered where there is an accumulation of opportunity and other red flags.

* SUMMARY POINTS OF CHAPTER 4 *

* Relationships with outside parties that make fraud easier to commit are:
    1) related-party transactions
    2) use of several different auditing firms or the frequent changing of auditors
    3) reluctance to give auditors needed data
    4) use of several different legal firms or the frequent changing of legal counsels
    5) use of a large number of banks
    6) continuous problems with regulatory agencies.
* Organizational structures that make fraud easier to commit are:
    1) complex business structures
    2) ineffective or nonexistent internal auditing staff
    3) high level of computerization in a firm
    4) inadequate internal controls
    5) rapid turnover of key employees.
* An economic environment that makes fraud easier to commit is its existence in an atypical or "hot" industry.
* Accounting practices that make fraud easier to commit are:
    1) large year-end or unusual transactions
    2) unduly liberal accounting practices
    3) poor accounting records
    4) inadequate staffing in the accounting department
    5) inadequate disclosure of questionable or unusual accounting practices.

5

PERSONAL
CHARACTERISTICS
THAT LEAD
TO FRAUD

This chapter examines personal characteristics that appear to be related to fraud. Many discussions of fraud have created a mistaken impression about the kinds of people who commit it. Since fraud is a criminal act, it is easy to assume that all fraud perpetrators are hardened career criminals. However, this false assumption overlooks the fact that most fraud perpetrators are not much different from other people in society. The personality profiles of fraud perpetrators are more similar to the profiles of average citizens than those of people convicted of other types of crimes.

People who commit fraud do not form a common profile with clearly-defined personality traits. The research examining criminal careers is reviewed later in Chapter 9 and the Appendices. The evidence seems to indicate that the best personal characteristic predicting fraudulent behavior is *a lack of personal integrity*. People with low personal integrity are more likely to commit fraud, regardless of other personality traits such as achievement, aggressiveness, and sociability. Procedures for measuring personal integrity are discussed in Chapter 9. This chapter describes eight personal characteristics related to a lack of integrity. These factors have been mentioned frequently in the literature on fraud.

While a lack of personal integrity contributes to fraud, it

should be remembered that fraud is also caused by convenient opportunities and situational pressures. The interaction of these three forces was mentioned in Chapter 2 and will be discussed more completely in Chapters 9 and 10. Many authors have argued that low personal integrity is a necessary condition for fraud; individuals have to be prone to dishonesty before situational pressures or opportunities can entice them to commit fraud. Whether or not there is a certain threshold of dishonesty required for fraud is unknown. Certainly, some individuals who have been convicted of fraud have had impressive records of honesty and fairness. Some of the prisoners we interviewed argued that their personal integrity was very high and that they only succumbed to fraud because of overwhelming pressures. Apparently some fraud perpetrators have had fairly high levels of personal integrity. Many frauds, however, have been committed by individuals with low integrity and a history of dishonest activities. The following eight factors are the most frequently-mentioned characteristics of individuals who commit fraud. While they are not easy to define or detect, these characteristics should be examined in order to assess the probability of fraud.

1. A person with low moral character
2. A person who rationalizes his contradictory behavior
3. A person without a strong code of personal ethics
4. A person who is a "wheeler-dealer"
5. A person lacking stability
6. A person with a strong desire to beat the system
7. A person who has a criminal or questionable background
8. A person with a poor credit rating and/or financial status.

LOW MORAL CHARACTER

Individuals who commit fraud have often been described as people who have low moral character. This description usually refers to a willingness to compromise a standard of honesty and choose what is expedient. People with low moral character do not consistently behave according to general rules defining what is fair and just. Instead, they choose what is advantageous to them in the immediate present, with little regard to future consequences, whether the action is right or wrong.

Nettler (1974) indicated that criminologists have hypothesized that one of the causes of crime is a general lack of moral character. Leibholz (1974) stated that an individual with deceptive or dishonest tendencies is a major security risk. Pecar (1975) believed fraud perpetrators have weak moral principles, while DiTullio (1969) described them as having only slight moral sensibilities. Geis (1968) pointed out that there are people who value money or profit above ethics, honesty, morality, and other ideals. Morris (1935) said that people are more honest in some situations than in others, indicating that most people are selective in their honesty and morality. While it is very difficult to measure, most agree that a person with low moral character is more likely to commit fraud than others. Perhaps the best indication of low moral character is a consistent trend of choosing what is expedient, with total disregard for what is legal or fair. Such an observation would require a prolonged period of interaction.

RATIONALIZATION OF CONTRADICTORY BEHAVIOR

The tendency to rationalize illegal or dishonest behavior is another indication of low moral character. The attitudes and rationalizations of embezzlers are as important as their motives in understanding fraud. The third item of Cressey's (1950) theory on embezzlement was that perpetrators must be able to rationalize their dishonesty in their own minds. This rationalization allows them to resolve their contradictory behavior and permits them to view what they are doing as "not wrong." This rationalization allows them to violate their positions of trust and still have that violation be consistent with their concept of themselves as honest people. Cressey also found that often the criminal had the attitude that others would understand if they "knew how much I needed it." Jaspan (1972) and Spencer (1965) indicated that one of the excuses for fraud seems to be "everybody's doing it, why single me out?" Morgenson (1975) stated that some perpetrators rationalize that "all people steal when they get in a tight spot." Morgenson also stated that some perpetrators rationalize that "honesty is the best policy, but business is business." The act in some way becomes "okay," because the perpetrator really needs this particular item. So what does an auditor look for? He can't simply ask "Do you rationalize?"

The tendency to rationalize is a difficult characteristic to define and observe. A single observation would not normally be adequate to label someone a rationalizer, but an auditor should be suspicious if a person frequently expresses opinions that are intended to justify or excuse improper actions on their part or within the company. Such justifications as "everyone is doing it," "it's a common practice," or "I don't think anyone would really care that much if they knew," are indications that a person is more likely to commit a fraud and rationalize the act.

LACK OF A STRONG CODE OF ETHICS

Quinney (1964) indicated that businessmen are more likely to commit fraud than are people in the professions. This is attributed to the fact that the ethical values taught by and expected of the professions are not similarly expected of businessmen. Reimer (1941), in analyzing 100 embezzlers, found that 23 were in public office and 35 in private business, indicating that these two fields are overrepresented. Baumhart (1961) felt that information regarding situational influences, as they relate to dishonest behavior, may have considerable value in developing hypotheses and strategies for studying fraud. In order to study these influences, he administered an extensive questionnaire to businessmen. From his research, he concluded that executives believe that a man with a well-defined personal code will be more likely to act ethically.

A "WHEELER-DEALER"

Forbes magazine (Blustein, 1978) published an article in which a lawyer, famous for his success in representing embezzlers, was interviewed. In talking about one particular individual, the substance of his comments was that his client was totally different in one respect from the typical white-collar criminal. The typical white-collar criminal is a gregarious guy, whereas his client was kind of introverted. He doesn't even drink. This indicates that from the lawyer's experience at least, most embezzlers are extroverted, fun-loving, sociable individuals. However, this category of "wheeler-dealer" is not limited to someone who is sociable or gregarious. It also includes someone who enjoys the feeling of power, influence, social status, and the excitement associated with rapid financial transactions involving large sums of money. DiTullio (1969) describes fraud perpetrators as imaginative and having an exaggerated sense of personality. Mannerheim (1965), in his study of thirty English embezzlers, found that most of them were ready and willing to take risks. Freedman (1973) also listed this risk-taking characteristic as suggesting a high probability of fraud. This personality trait is also supported by two of our authors who have worked with fraud perpetrators in prison.

An empirical study comparing embezzlers with other criminals conducted by Eysenck, Rust, and Eysenck (1977) found that they scored lowest of all groups on both psychosis and neurosis, while scoring high on extroversion. Extroversion is a major personality trait of the wheeler-dealer. In this sense, they set themselves apart from other criminal groups, appearing to be more like non-offenders.

As an example, in the Salad Oil case, De Angelis was known for his chauffer-driven Cadillac, his big deals, and his free-spending habits. He was forever pressing cash into the hands of his many admirers. In the Equity Funding case, Roger B, one of the company's founders, was a wealthy, fast-living person. He had a spectrum of friends ranging from bar derelicts to Wall Street financiers. He loved one hundred mile-per-hour spins in his Lincoln Continental and was often found at parties. Equity's president moved the company to the twenty-eighth floor of the Century City Building, where his office was complete with a fireplace, reception room, bathroom, and kitchen, as well as an extensive view of Beverly Hills.

INSTABILITY

The most common, basic causes of negative life-style patterns resulting in instability are (1) promotional stagnation, (2) career plateauing, (3) the aging syndrome, and (4) domestic incompatibility (Gorrill, 1974 and Reimer, 1941). These four conditions may be interrelated and are likely to lead to frustration and dishonesty on the job.

In a rather thorough analysis of security procedures, Gorrill suggested that all factors relative to stability need to be checked out carefully. For example, marital status may provide evidence of a problem in stability or maturity. A criminal background investigation might also reveal certain problems in adjustment. It is not a divorce or a criminal record per se that is important, but they are additional indications of instability. The ongoing problems of key employees must be assessed in identifying problem personnel or potential fraud perpetrators. In fact, the presence of personality or behavioral instability usually leads to employment problems, even though the perpetrators have never been divorced or convicted.

Gorrill (1974) presents ten points to ponder in assessing background factors that would be predictive of instability:

1. Frequent job changes
2. Unsatisfactory employment
3. Periods of unemployment
4. Frequent changes of residence
5. Gambling and drinking problems
6. Financial overinvolvement
7. Marital problems
8. Excessive education above immediate or projected requirements for the job
9. Involvement in illegal activities
10. Falsification of the employment application.

There are many additional, work-related factors that may be useful in a preliminary assessment of fraud potential. A crisis late in one's career may precipitate an unusual or deviant act (Reimer, 1941). In this same vein, Reimer also suggested that many job changes or the failure of the individual's own business, necessitating a return to working for someone else, may trigger a problem.

DESIRE TO BEAT THE SYSTEM

A common finding, especially in analyzing computer criminals, is that a perpetrator of fraud is often motivated by the intellectual challenge presented by the fraud opportunity (Parker, 1975; DeGouw, 1978; Gottheimer, 1978; Meyers, 1975; Freed, 1969; Norman, 1976; Podgus, 1973; Nycum, 1975). Many individuals in the computer industry are there because they find the equipment, programming, operating systems, and other factors extremely interesting and challenging. Some of the most successful of these technicians are insatiably curious and love to dig in and figure out how the latest thing works, and one of the latest things is data-processing security. Many people involved with computers seem to thrive on these challenges, which are often much more interesting than the normal workday assignments of the systems technician. The technician could easily find himself thinking, "I will figure out how they think they have made this system secure, break that security, and prove, at least to myself, my superior technical capabilities." For many technicians, this challenge may well be a greater enticement to systems manipulation than the possibility of financial gain. Once tempted by this kind of gamesmanship, the computer criminal can become enthralled and finally entrapped by a kind of impersonal numbers game, in which the moral implications of fraud are lost (Gottheimer, 1978). In essence, some authors feel that the technicians can't be fully satisfied by their intellectual accomplishments until they have actually "beaten the system." The solution to this problem has been said to lie in directing the personal challenge back into the job itself by enriching it (Carson, 1977; Herzberg, 1976; Zeitlin, 1971).

As an example, one of Equity Funding's programmers gave notice in December of 1971 that he was quitting because of boredom. At that point, he was recruited by a high official to develop a computer system for the insurance against fraud, a position which he gratefully accepted. Not only would it be exciting, but he got a raise of $100 per month and an opportunity to buy Equity Funding stock at special prices (Cardoso, 1974).

Another example is Jimmy S., a highly-motivated young fraud perpetrator, who was arrested in Los Angeles in 1972. He was charged with stealing what police estimated as a million dollars worth of electronic equipment from Pacific Telephone and Telegraph Company (Gottheimer, 1978). Jimmy S. was fascinated by computers throughout high school and by the age of twenty-one, he had set up his own business as an independent supplier of telephone equipment. One day while walking home from high school, he passed a Pacific Telephone Supply storeroom and noticed a trash can filled with papers of various sorts. He rummaged through them and discovered that they included parts manuals and operating guides for the telephone company's computers. He began to wander past this storeroom more often and, over a period of time, he built up a technical library from the materials salvaged from the trash cans. Eventually, the library included management guides detailing how Pacific telephone ordered equipment from Western Electric Company. Several years later, he put this library to use. He was able to penetrate Pacific Telephone's computer system and order equipment for himself. He put in requisitions for the equipment he wanted, then had it delivered to isolated locations where he would arrange to have it picked up. He continued these operations for several months without incident until January of 1972, when his activities were reported by one of his employees who had been refused a salary increase. The employee went to the police, Jerry S.'s warehouse was raided, and he was arrested. After serving 40 days in jail, he was released and soon established a profitable business as a computer security consultant, providing inside knowledge of how to prevent computer crime.

CRIMINAL OR QUESTIONABLE BACKGROUND

An empirical study conducted by the authors (see Appendix C) revealed that there appear to be two types of fraud perpetrators: (1) those with no previous criminal history who succumb to pressures and temptations and (2) the chronic criminal type who engages in fraud as just another in a series of dishonest acts. Supporting the first type, Parker (1975) profiled computer fraud perpetrators and found that a great majority of them had no past criminal background. The *Corporate Treasurer's and Controller's Encyclopedia* (Lillian, 1958) indicated that in a large majority of fraud cases,

> . . . the person committing the fraud is an employee with many years of service and one whose faithful devotion to duty has won him the respect of his employer and steady promotions to more and more responsibilities. In most instances, he is highly regarded by his office associates and is a pillar of his community. Furthermore, the man or woman who defrauds his employer usually is a first offender. Only rarely does the perpetrator of corporate fraud have a criminal record. Consequently, previous police, court, or prison records are not usually available to act as a warning of possible dishonest conduct.

Supporting the second type, Rose (1975) indicated that of the sixty-five fraud offenders he studied, 12.3 percent had been investigated or convicted on previous occasions for other offenses. Coopers and Lybrand (1977) indicated that auditors should be alert to executives with records of malfeasance or with shady backgrounds.

As an example, a couple of years before the case came to court, Homestake Production and its president signed a statement at the SEC's request that they would refrain from all future fraudulent activities. One of the principals of the Black Watch Farms, Inc. had been accused of criminal activity on several different occasions prior to his participation in that embezzlement. Philip Musica of McKesson Robbins had been arrested twice for fraudulent activities in business before his involvement in McKesson Robbins. In 1909, he was arrested for bribing customs officers to certify that his father's cheese weighed less than its actual weight, and again in 1913, when the supposed $25,000 collateral he had put up on a bank loan for U.S. Hair Co. was actually $250 worth of trash hair. Tino De Angelis had a notable history of fraud and deception. Reports stated that his wartime success was based on black market sales, and accusations arose concerning the export of substandard cooking fat to Yugoslavia. For this offense he was required to pay $100,000 in damages. In 1950, the Republic of

Italy sued De Angelis, charging fraudulent misrepresentation in connection with the purchase of tallow. When in control of the Adolph Gobel meat-packing company, numerous allegations of inferior products and short deliveries were made concerning his sales to the government-aided school lunch program. In 1953, the Securities and Exchange Commission placed Adolph Gobel in receivership when allegations of understated losses in Gobel's published accounts appeared. Another one of De Angelis' companies was charged, shortly after the Adolph Gobel incident, of exporting inferior lard to Germany and damages of $100,000 were again paid. Other incidents involving Adolph Gobel included: falsified shipping papers under the "Food for Peace" program, $1.5 million of personal income tax evasion, and fake inventories at Adolph Gobel. The first two were settled out of court and the third charge was dropped when the key prosecution witness mysteriously changed his mind about the evidence and suffered a prolonged bout of "assisted" amnesia. After Adolph Gobel went bankrupt, De Angelis organized Allied Crude Vegetable Oil Refining Corporation. In 1958, Allied was sued by the government for having wrongly collected $1.2 million in Agriculture Department funds on a shipment of soybean oil to Spain. After having paid $1.5 million to settle a claim with the "Food for Peace" program, Allied was again suspended when it shipped 437 million pounds of vegetable oils and shortenings in leaky containers, causing much of the oil to become rancid. Senator Williams of Delaware stated that the $70 million shipment was worthless. In 1980, De Angelis was accused of masterminding another major fraud. This time the company was "Mr. Pork" and the city was Indianapolis, but many other factors remain the same. *The Wall Street Journal* (1980) states: "And instead of selling 1.8 billion pounds of oil that didn't exist, this time he's accused of selling thousands of little pigs that did exist—without paying for them."

Other recent examples of questionable background are a chief executive officer of a major life insurance company who had twice before faced charges relating to the misuse of insurance company funds; an officer of another corporation who had previously pleaded guilty to a securities fraud and served a three-month jail term; an officer of a corporation who had previously been sentenced to 90 days in prison after pleading guilty to stock fraud and had twice been enjoined from further violation by the SEC; and an officer of still another corporation, who had previously been disbarred as an attorney and convicted of swindling $65,000 from a Miami bank when he was its counsel and a director. All four of these individuals were involved in major frauds in their companies.

POOR CREDIT RATING OR FINANCIAL STATUS

Burnstein (1959) and Leibholz and Wilson (1974) list a poor credit rating as an indicator of embezzlement. Kintzele and Kintzele (1976) stated that employers should be careful about an individual who is constantly being chased by creditors or collectors, because this person has a greater motivation to commit fraud. Levens (1964) stated that 75 of the 97 embezzlers he studied were in financial difficulty. Reimer (1941) listed several financial problems that can contribute to fraud: a family conflict where it appears that more money would lead to happiness and a resolution of the conflict; overindebtedness; impending bankruptcy, and money "borrowed" from the company with the intention of replacing it before it is detected. Reimer supported his point by stating that 88 out of 100 embezzlers studied were under financial strain, and only 4 of 100 cases were related to the desire for amusement or leisure consumption.

VALIDATION OF PERSONAL CHARACTERISTIC RED FLAGS

In this chapter, personal characteristic factors that make one more inclined to commit fraud were discussed. These red flags have been examined in the context of 52 fraud cases, and a summary of the results of that comparative analysis is presented in Table 3 of Appendix D. The table shows that all of the red flags discussed can be associated with at least one major fraud.

* SUMMARY POINTS OF CHAPTER 5 *

* There is no single personal characteristic that causes fraud. Rather, fraud is committed by all types of people in most occupations.
* Personal and psychological characteristics that suggest a high probability of fraud are:
    1) low moral character
    2) rationalization of contradictory behavior
    3) a lack of a strong code of ethics
    4) wheeler-dealing
    5) a lack of stability (associated with promotional stagnation, career plateauing, aging, or domestic incompatibility
    6) a strong desire to beat the system.
* Demographic characteristics that suggest a high probability of fraud are:
    1) criminal or questionable background; and
    2) poor credit rating or financial status.

6

A RISK EVALUATION APPROACH TO PREVENTING AND DETECTING FRAUD

Chapter 6 Contains:

- A practical checklist for preventing and controlling fraud.

$\mathbf{B}$ecause of the enormous cost of fraud, it is important for auditors to examine the variables identified in our model (situational pressures, opportunities, and personal characteristics). Chapter 6 contains a comprehensive checklist that includes all of the red flags discussed in Appendices B and C.

This checklist represents a deviation from current audit and management control practices. However, there is already a trend toward these types of procedures. Both Touche Ross (1974), Coopers & Lybrand (1977), and the AICPA (SAS 6 and 16) have reported red flag lists which identify situational pressures in a firm that can signal potential fraud. To our knowledge, however, no such lists exist for personal situational pressure, opportunity, or personal characteristic factors.

We appreciate the difficulty of completing this checklist. Many of the questions are extremely sensitive and previously have been thought to be of no concern to either auditors or management. However, all of the elements included in the questions have been associated with past frauds, and we believe that they can indicate the possible existence of fraud in the future.

The questionnaire has been designed so that a "yes" response indicates an area of concern. Upon completing the questionnaire, auditors and managers should give careful consideration to the reasons underlying these responses. While single, or even many, "yes" answers do not guarantee the existence of fraud, the probability increases as "yes" answers become more frequent, more serious, or more unjustified.

This questionnaire can provide two major benefits for auditors and managers, in both business and government agencies. First, it will greatly assist auditors and managers in deterring and preventing fraud. Second, it will create a greater awareness of the possibility of fraud being committed by employees and clients.

FRAUD RISK EVALUATION QUESTIONNAIRE

SITUATIONAL PRESSURES

A.   Individuals Against the Company

Questions	Yes	No	N/A
1. Do any of the key employees have unusually high personal debts or financial losses (i.e., high enough that they probably could not meet them with their own level of income)?			
2. Do any of the key employees appear to be receiving incomes that are inadequate to cover normal personal and family expenses?			
3. Do any of the key employees appear to be living beyond their means?			
4. Are any of the key employees involved in extensive stock-market or other speculation (i.e., extensive enough so that a downturn would cause them severe financial difficulty)?			
5. Are any of the key employees involved in excessive or habitual gambling?			

6. Do any of the key employees have unusually high expenses resulting from personal involvement with other people (e.g., maintenance of separate apartments)?

7. Do any of the key employees feel undue family, community, or social expectations or pressures?

8. Do any of the key employees use alcohol or drugs excessively?

9. Do any of the key employees strongly believe that they are being treated unfairly (e.g., underpaid, poor job assignments)?

10. Do any of the key employees appear to resent their superiors?

11. Are any of the key employees unduly frustrated with their jobs?

12. Is there an undue amount of peer pressure to achieve in this company, so much so that success is more important than ethics?

13. Do any of the key employees appear to exhibit extreme greed or an overwhelming desire for self-enrichment or personal gain?

B.   Individuals on Behalf of the Company

Questions	Yes	No	N/A
14. Has the company recently experienced severe losses from any major investments or ventures?			
15. Is the company attempting to operate with insufficient working capital?			

16. Does the company have unusually high debts, so high that either interest payments or balances due impose a threat to the stability of the company?

17. Have tight credit or high interest rates reduced the company's ability to acquire credit? Is there undue pressure to finance expansion through current earnings rather than through debt or equity?

18. Is the company caught in a profit squeeze, (i.e., are costs and expenses rising higher and faster than sales and revenues)?

19. Do existing loan agreements provide little available tolerance on debt restrictions?

20. Has the company's quality of earnings been progressively deteriorating (e.g., adopting straight-line depreciation to replace an accelerated depreciation without good reason, or reporting good profits but experiencing cash shortages)?

21. Is the company experiencing an urgent need to report favorable earnings (e.g., to support a high stock price or to meet forecasted earnings?

22. Does company management believe there is a need to gloss over a "temporarily bad situation" in order to maintain management position and prestige?

23. Does the company have a significant amount of unmarketable collateral?

24. Does the company depend heavily on only one or two products, customers, or transactions?

25. Does the company have an excess of idle productive capacity?

26. Does the company suffer from severe obsolesence, (i.e., is a significant amount of inventory or physical facilities obsolete)?

27. Does the company have an unusually long business cycle, long enough so that profits or cash flows are threatened?

28. Does the company have any revocable or possibly imperiled licenses that are necessary for the firm's existence or continued operation?

29. Has the company expanded rapidly through new business or product lines? If so, has expansion been orderly or has it been done in an attempt to salvage profitability?

30. Are there currently, or have there recently been unfavorable economic conditions within this company's industry, or is the company's performance running counter to industry trends?

31. Is the company experiencing undue difficulty in collecting receivables, (i.e., is the receivable turnover slowing down)?

32. Does the company face unusually heavy competition, heavy enough that its existence appears threatened?

33. Is the company experiencing a significant reduction in sales backlog, indicating a future decline in sales?

34. Is the company being pressured to either sell out or merge with another company?

35. Is the company experiencing sizable inventory increases without comparable sales increases?

36. Has the company recently experienced any significant adverse tax adjustments or changes?

37. Is the company experiencing significant litigation, especially between stockholders and management?

61

38. Has the company recently been suspended or delisted from a stock exchange?

OPPORTUNITIES

C. Individuals Against the Company

Questions	Yes	No	N/A
39. Do any of the key employees have close associations with suppliers or key individuals who might have motives inconsistent with the company's welfare?			
40. Does the company fail to inform employees about rules of personal conduct and the discipline of fraud perpetrators?			
41. Is the company experiencing a rapid turnover of key employees, either through their quitting or being fired?			

145
146

42. Have any of the key employees recently failed to take annual vacations of more than one or two days, or has the company failed to periodically rotate or transfer key personnel?

43. Does the company have inadequate personnel screening policies when hiring new employees to fill positions of trust? (e.g., check on secondary references, etc.)?

44. Does the company lack explicit and uniform personnel policies?

45. Does the company fail to maintain accurate personnel records of dishonest acts or disciplinary actions?

46. Does the company fail to require executive disclosures and examinations (e.g., personal investments or incomes)?

47. Does the company appear to have dishonest or unethical management?

48. Is the company dominated by only one or two individuals?

49. Does the company appear to operate continually on a crisis basis?

50. Does the company fail to pay attention to details? (e.g., are accurate accounting records unimportant)?

51. Does the company place too much trust in key employees and overlook traditional controls?

52. Is there a lack of good interpersonal relationships among the key executives in the company?

53. Does the company have unrealistic productivity measurements or expectations?

54. Does the company have poor compensation practices? Is pay commensurate with the level of responsibility?

55. Does the company lack a good system of internal security (e.g., locks, safes, fences, gates, and guards)?

56. Does the company lack adequate training programs?

57. Does the company have an inade-
158 quate internal control system, or does it fail to enforce the existing controls?

D. Individuals on Behalf of the Company

Questions	Yes	No	N/A

58. Has the company recently had any
66 significant related-party transactions?

59. Does the company retain different
67 auditing firms for major subsidiaries, or does it change auditors often?

60. Is the company reluctant to provide
71 the auditors with data needed to complete the audit examination?

61. Does the company retain several different legal counsels, or does it change legal counsels often?

62. Does the company use several dif-
72 ferent banks, none of which can see the company's entire financial picture?

63. Does the company seem to have continuous problems with regulatory agencies?

64. Does the company possess an unduly complex business structure, so complex that many facets lack purpose or meaning?

65. Does the company seem to need but lack an effective internal auditing staff?

66. Is the company highly computerized? If so, are there insufficient controls over hardware, software, computer personnel, etc.?

67. Does the company have an inadequate internal control system, or does it fail to enforce the existing internal controls?

68. Is the company in a "hot" or high-risk industry (i.e., an industry which has experienced a large number of business failures or frauds)?

69. Does the company have a number of large year-end or unusual transactions?

70. Does the company have unduly liberal accounting practices?

71. Does the company have poor accounting records?

72. Does the accounting department of the company appear to be inadequately staffed?

73. Does the company fail to disclose questionable or unusual accounting practices?

E. Personal Characteristics

Questions	Yes	No	N/A
74. Do any of the key employees appear to have low moral characters?			
75. When confronted with difficulty, do any of the key employees appear to consistently rationalize contradictory behavior?			
76. Do any of the key employees appear to lack a strong personal code of honesty?			
77. Do any of the key employees appear to be "wheeler-dealers"—individuals who enjoy feelings of power, influence, social status, and excitement associated with financial transactions involving large sums of money?			
78. Do any of the key employees appear to be unstable (e.g., frequent job changes, frequent changes of residence, mental problems)?			
79. Do any of the key employees appear to be intrigued by the personal challenge of subverting a system of controls (i.e., do they appear to have a desire to beat the system)?			
80. Do any key employees have criminal or questionable backgrounds?			
81. Do any of the key employees have poor credit ratings?			
82. Do any of the key employees have poor past work records or references?			

Explanations of Yes Answers

No. ____ _____
_____
_____

No. ____ _____
_____
_____

No. ____ _____
_____
_____

No. ____ _____
_____
_____

Chart 6–1

CONCLUSION

Our model of fraud has focused on the interaction of three major forces—*situational pressures, opportunities,* and *personal integrity (or honesty)*. Societal factors provide a base upon which these forces function which contributes to the fraud problem. The list of fraud-related variables is not final or complete; additional elements will be discovered, and the categories will be expanded. However, we are confident that the model presented here is a needed step to bring some order out of chaos. The mountains of material written about fraud have been reduced to a manageable mound.

Understanding the phenomenon of fraud, detecting it, and preventing it have been the intentions of this effort. A first line of defense will rely on management strategies and accounting procedures. Auditors can more adequately aid in the protection against dishonesty if properly equipped. The interview questionnaire resulting from this analysis will hopefully provide such a tool against fraud.

Fraud, the crime of the 80s, looms large as a dominant factor afflicting our life-style, which is being victimized by encroaching dishonesty and illegal activities. Businesses cannot survive the upward trend of this internal destructiveness perpetrated by individuals and groups for whatever reasons. Our very economy stands in danger of collapse from dishonesty, waste, manipulation, and losses that force an ever-increasing number of companies out of business and into less productive existences. Moral disintegration is another considerable loss. The "danger-from-within " is real and gigantic in proportion. Everyone is affected by fraud, though it be an unseen enemy for the most part.

We trust this work will contribute in a small but significant way to the fight against fraud. Ultimate success will require a concerted, ongoing effort, aimed at improving business practices and people.

SECTION III

STRATEGIES FOR REDUCING EMPLOYEE FRAUD

7

HOW TO REDUCE SITUATIONAL PRESSURES ON EMPLOYEES

Chapter 7 Explains:

- Why personal pressures lead to fraud.
- Rationalizations for committing fraud.
- Financial pressures that can lead to fraud.
- Habits that can lead to fraud.
- Feelings that can lead to fraud.

If managers are sufficiently concerned about the possibilities of fraud in their companies, there are several actions they can take. The three major causes of fraud were explained earlier in Chapter 2. These three causes include situational pressures, convenient opportunities, and a lack of personal integrity. A careful examination of these three causes provides a useful framework for diagnosing fraud and taking corrective action to reduce it.

In short, fraud is reduced by lessening the pressures and opportunities to commit it, and by increasing personal integrity. If managers hope to effectively reduce fraud, they must (a) be aware of the situational pressures compelling employees to commit fraud and reduce them where possible, (b) identify the opportunities that make fraud very convenient and eliminate unnecessary convenience, and (c) be able to select individuals with high levels of moral integrity to occupy important positions of trust, and to create an environment that contributes to greater integrity. These three strategies are discussed in this and the next two chapters.

Some of the recommended ways of reducing fraud may not be very popular. Some issues are very sensitive and certain questions that ought to be asked may seem like an invasion of personal privacy. Managers should only adopt changes that seem necessary for their particular situation. As the potential losses from fraud or the opportunities to commit fraud increase, more factors ought to be considered.

Situational pressures do not really cause people to commit fraud. Regardless of the pressures they face, individuals can still choose to behave honestly. Employees have the free agency to choose for themselves whether they will act honestly and uprightly or whether they will embezzle, steal, or misrepresent. Some people face tremendous pressures and do not resort to fraud.

On the other hand, many white-collar criminals claim that the reason they committed fraud was because of the pressures they faced. For some of them, the situational pressures were so intense that they had to act, and fraud was the only feasible solution, or at least the most satisfactory solution for the present time. "I'm as honest as the next fellow," said an inmate serving time in prison for fraud, "but I was backed up against the wall. I didn't have any other alternative." The presence of some sort of intense pressure is frequently observed in cases of white-collar crime. In fact, a typical response of most white-collar criminals is, "If you could only appreciate the position I was in, you would understand why I did it."

Situational pressures can be created by many things, including circumstances at work, conditions at home, personal habits and appetites, and other factors in an individual's personal life. The only common element in all these situations is that they all involve a financial strain.

Intense pressure can be created by unique personal situations. One woman, for example, was convicted for embezzling $50,000 from her employer. The woman did not want her daughter going to prison since she would be left to care for the children. "I just didn't have the patience or interest to be a good guardian to those kids; they needed their mother. I decided it would be better for me to go to jail than her." Another woman was convicted of fraud when she embezzled money to cover the checks her husband wrote. After a marital squabble, he went on a spending spree and she felt compelled to cover the checks he had written.

The desire to serve the community or protect society can even be interpreted as a pressure that contributes to fraud. A man spending time in prison for fraud said his conviction resulted from trying to keep his own store and other nearby shops from going bankrupt. "When the interstate was finished, we lost most of our business. We knew some of it would return, especially if we put together some good advertising. But in the meantime, we were losing a lot of money and a lot of people were soon going to be out of work."

The influence of intense situational pressures such as these have generally been overlooked in efforts to reduce fraud. Managers and auditors have directed most of their fraud detection efforts toward controlling opportunities to commit fraud against the company. Audit checklists and red flag lists (e.g., Touche Ross, Coopers & Lybrand, and the AICPA, especially SAS 6 and 16) have concentrated on two areas: (a) economic factors that motivate management to commit fraud on behalf of the company, and (b) organizational processes indicating that businesses are deliberately designed to commit fraud. These lists overlook the possibility that key employees might be trying to cope with situational pressures that cause them to commit fraud for their own personal benefit. This chapter examines the situational pressures that motivate individuals to commit fraud.

Donald Cressey, a noted scholar on fraud, has developed a well-known explanation for fraud that recognizes the influences of situational pressures. Cressey's theory suggests that trusted persons become trust violators when: (1) they conceive of themselves as having a financial problem that is not solvable in a socially-sanctioned manner and is therefore not sharable; (2) they have the knowledge or awareness that this problem can be secretly resolved by violation of the position of financial trust; and (3) they are able to apply to their own conduct in that situation a rationalization enabling them to adjust their concepts of themselves as trusted persons, to their concepts of themselves as users of the entrusted funds or property (i.e., they are able to rationalize their misconduct). Cressey claimed that unless all three conditions were present, the trusted person did not become a trust violator. In discussing management fraud, numerous other authors have agreed with Cressey and have referred to his work (Catlett, 1974; Morgenson, 1975; Gilson, 1975; and Freedman, 1973). Donn Parker's study of computer criminals also showed that a great deal of computer crime seems to spring from traditional motives such as a financial need.

More recently, in discussing management fraud, Barnett (1978) asked the question, "What causes an educated, seemingly intelligent business or professional person to cheat and risk prison when that person never before had ventured from the straight and narrow?" He answered the question by quoting Dr. Barbara Bliss, a former psychiatrist at the McNeil Island maximum security penitentiary. Dr. Bliss claimed that fraud is a solution to a problem, and people will turn to it when they become desperate. She stated that fraud perpetrators rarely act impulsively; that is, they don't pick up a gun and rob a bank to get money. Instead, they plan the crime so that there is no violence and therefore less danger. They also know that if they get caught, they will probably get less time than if they went after the money with a gun.

The U. S. Chamber of Commerce (1974) stated that some people, while initially honest, become subject to pressures originating outside the firm and resort to various forms of dishonesty to solve those problems. Pecar (1975) indicated that Soviet criminal literature also stresses financial or other needs as the motivating mechanism for committing fraud.

Situational pressures are not unique to a specific group of people. Intense pressures can create stress for anyone and it is difficult to predict who will perceive fraud as the only solution to the problem. The personal characteristics, the background, the job status, the motives, and the economic position of perpetrators seem to be as varied as humanity itself (Jefferey, 1970; Kintzele and Kintzele, 1976). Occasionally it is quite surprising to discover that a particular person has committed a fraud. In a large majority of fraud and embezzlement cases, the person committing the fraud is a key employee with many years of service. The employee is often one whose faithful devotion to duty has won the respect of the employer and steady promotions giving increasing responsibility (Lillian, 1968; Comer, 1977). In most instances, the perpetrator is highly regarded by associates and is a pillar of the community. Furthermore, the man or woman who defrauds an employer is usually a first-time offender. Only rarely does the perpetrator of corporate fraud have a criminal record. Consequently, there are no previous police, court, or prison records, which could warn of possible future dishonesty. Nor is the corporate defrauder the commonly-perceived criminal type, since such people are usually not employed at managerial or executive levels in business.

An extremely intense source of situational pressure can be created by the individual's perception of social expectations. Barnett (1978) indicated that most fraud perpetrators are family men with high status in the community. When they become overextended or suffer a financial reversal, they see not only themselves but also their family members losing their positions of status. Their wives will have to give up their carefree lifestyles, they will have to drop out of the country club, and the kids can no longer afford to go to private schools. Barnett also indicated that, since most of these people are go-getters who have built up businesses, they can't bear to see it all go down the drain. He quoted Dr. Bliss as saying that once an offender winds up in prison, his biggest regret is what he has done to his family. Often the home and possessions have to be sacrificed, since a perpetrator engaged in criminal activity at that level gambles for hundreds of thousands of dollars and is destroyed if he loses.

Cressey (1951) indicated that embezzlers must be able to apply a rationalization to their conduct, which enables them to adjust their self-concept as trusted persons, to their self-concept as users of the entrusted funds or property. There are numerous rationalizations. Many embezzlers do not initially intend to steal—instead they explain their actions as "borrowing" from their companies. They intend to restore the "borrowed" money before the theft is discovered. Unfortunately, all too often the individuals get "involved" and must borrow larger and larger amounts of money in order to meet their needs, and are never able to repay the "loan." Many perpetrators contend that they really didn't intend to break the law. Instead, they got swept up in a pressure-cooked, fast-paced business world and were forced into a corner.

Other fraud perpetrators rationalize their acts by claiming

that "honesty is the best policy, but business is business," "it's only a machine or computer," "it's a large organization and no one will be hurt by my actions," or "everybody is doing it, so why not me?" Other fraud perpetrators try to justify their actions by claiming that they are "only small deviations and really aren't illegal" or "all people steal when they are in a tight spot, so what I'm doing is really not wrong." Others rationalize by saying that the employer owes them the money, so "I'm only taking what is rightfully mine," or that "I had no other choice." Some feel that "people would understand if they only knew how much I needed it." Some perpetrators, when caught, blame management: "It isn't my fault, you forced me to do it by. . . ."

There are numerous situational pressures that might motivate an individual to resort to fraud. Our review of the literature on fraud indicates that the following pressures were the most frequently-mentioned forms of situational pressures. These situational pressures are items Cressey might have labeled non-sharable needs that are not solvable in socially-sanctioned ways.

1. High personal debts or financial losses
2. Inadequate incomes
3. Living beyond one's means
4. Extensive stock-market or other speculation
5. Excessive gambling
6. Involvement with members of the opposite sex
7. Undue family, community, or social expectations
8. Excessive use of alcohol or drugs
9. Perceived inequities in the organization
10. Corporate or peer-group pressures

HIGH PERSONAL DEBTS OR FINANCIAL LOSSES

People with serious financial problems are in a high-risk category and are more likely than others to turn to fraud as an answer to their problems. Reimer (1941) found that 88 of the 100 embezzlers he studied were under immediate financial strain. Embezzlement, in the great majority of cases, was seen as the only solution to severe economic strains such as the loss of a business, job, family, home, etc. Levens (1964) found that 75 of the 97 embezzlers he studied were in financial difficulty. Mannerheim (1965) studied 30 embezzlers in England and found that many viewed their fraudulent acts as the best way to avert their impending bankruptcy. Jefferey (1970), Kintzele and Kintzele (1976), Krause (1965), and the U. S. Chamber of Commerce (1974) also indicated that high personal debt and/or financial losses were motivations for perpetrators to commit fraudulent acts. As a related factor, the Chamber of Commerce (1974) also listed loan-shark involvement as a possible cause of fraud. Loan-shark involvement usually results from high personal debt or financial loss.

Owners of businesses that are in financial difficulty are more likely to commit fraud (Quinney, 1963). Reimer (1941) stated that criminal behavior grows most naturally out of the occupational routine where a private entrepreneur is struggling against bankruptcy, and where the means of delaying liquidation are not abundant. He claimed that in at least 33 of his 100 cases, a sequence of increasing debt led to the embezzlement. He found that another common occurrence was a fraud perpetrator who had many job changes in the hope of achieving financial independence in another setting. Many of these embezzlers had failed in their own businesses and had gone back to work for someone else. These setbacks at times shattered homes and destroyed families. In some instances, the indebtedness problem was compounded by the fact that the perpetrator was unwilling to admit the indebtedness to his family, and especially to his wife (Spencer, 1965; Cressey, 1950). In 1947, the Chicago Crime Commission studied the problem of business frauds and found five factors they felt were responsible for most frauds. One was unusual family expenses. Jefferey (1970) and Freedman (1973) also listed unusual family expenses as motivation for fraud.

An illustration of how financial losses can create enormous situational pressures is shown in the case of Raymond K., a grain elevator owner in Stockport, Iowa (*Wall Street Journal*, 1980). Raymond K. was the local boy who made good. He started out driving a coal truck, bought into an elevator in 1958, and made it a thriving business. He really struck it rich in the early 1970s, when he profited from trading grain on the commodities market. He built a lavish house on a bluff overlooking the Des Moines River, complete with an indoor swimming pool, a sauna, and a three-car garage. Raymond K. worked hard, sometimes from 5 a.m. to 11 p.m. during harvest, and he was generous, always extending credit to farmers in a bind and doing favors for others. In 1979, Raymond K., who attended a Christian Church, sent the pastor and his wife on a trip to the Holy Land, along with members of Raymond K.'s family.

Sometime in 1979, Raymond K.'s finances apparently took a turn for the worse. Signs that something was wrong at Prairie Grain surfaced in late December and early January. He asked some farmers to wait for their money, and he gave a few others bad checks. Most Stockport residents guessed that Raymond K. lost a lot of money playing the commodities markets, then was forced to embezzle the grain to cover his losses. Perhaps he may have been hurt by the embargo on grain sales to Russia. Immediately after the early-January problems, the grain pipeline virtually halted. Because of uncertainty, companies stopped buying from elevators and elevators stopped buying from farmers. Thus there was a cash-flow problem for a while, and, in addition, Raymond K. was deeply in debt. Two banks that were owed nearly $2.1 million in loans to Prairie Grain had called for payment. Five other banks made claims for loans ranging from $65,000 to $450,000.

On January 31, 1980, as a result of rumors about his losses and an unexpected visit from a state auditor, Raymond K. climbed into his pickup truck, drove seven miles outside of Stockport and put a bullet through his head. Thus, financial losses had taken the town's leading businessman, a devoted churchgoer, and a friend of nearly everyone for miles around.

INADEQUATE INCOMES

Lillian (1968) indicates that the earning of an inadequate income motivates fraud. Here, inadequate income does not refer to the demands arising from an extravagant life-style. It refers to actual or perceived insufficient money to enable employees to feed, house, and clothe their families according to their established standards. Long-term employees sometimes feel justified in embezzling on the grounds that their employer has been unfair and actually owes them the money they are stealing. For example, other younger employees may have been promoted before them. A deterrent to this type of fraud is the upward adjustment of the salaries of employees who are in positions of trust.

In Leven's (1964) study, perceived inadequate income was the second most prevalent reason (21 percent) given for the perpetrators' financial troubles. Reimer (1941) indicated that people with unstable, declining, or insecure careers are more likely than others to become involved in fraudulent activities. Baumhart (1961), Freedman (1973), and the Chicago Crime Commission (Curtis, 1960) also list inadequate income as a cause of fraudulent activity.

Sometimes company expectations or requirements lead an individual into fraudulent activity. If an employer requires employees to associate with a wealthy class of people for the purpose of increasing business, he should make certain that employees receive adequate salaries or expense allowances. Without an adequate salary or expense allowance, employees are usually unable to achieve the company-imposed objective and are faced with the decision of either not meeting the employer's requirement or finding other funds in order to achieve that objective (Lillian, 1968; Freedman, 1973).

LIVING BEYOND ONE'S MEANS

Severe financial pressures will ultimately occur when individuals adopt a higher standard of living than they can afford. Some surety companies attribute more of their losses to extravagant living standards than to any other cause. In some instances, extravagant living arises because of personal or family expectations (Lillian, 1968). Attempting to follow an expensive style of living that exceeds the individual's financial means of support has been identified frequently as an important potential contributor to fraud (Freedman (1973), Robertson (1973), Kintzele and Kintzele (1976), Reimer (1941), Curtis (1960), and Comer (1977)).

An example of extravagant living is seen in the case of a Penn Central executive who kept a bedroom and sauna at his office, an extra apartment in Manhattan, and had a number of girlfriends to support. Another illustration is the case of Kurt R. Before founding a student marketing corporation, Kurt R. worked for General Electric and ITT, and appeared to be a solid, stable, conservative employee. After founding the company, his life-style changed dramatically. He bought a Lear Jet, threw extravagant parties, bought a $600,000 home, developed very expensive tastes, and tried to portray himself as an elitist. Likewise, the stock fraud and collapse of P. T. Clark and Co. was attributed in part to extravagant living. They experienced a large cash drain for "extravagant and nonessential expenditures" including the leasing of 11 expensive automobiles (including two Rolls Royce Silver Clouds), two large pleasure boats, and $180,000 worth of antique furniture for an executive's home (WSJ, 1975).

STOCK MARKET OR OTHER SPECULATION

Another manner in which a critical, non-sharable financial need can arise is through extensive stock market speculation (U. S. Chamber of Commerce, 1974; (Lillian, 1968). In many cases, the perpetrator starts out with completely honest intentions. However, unwise investments, fed by desires to become wealthy, result in significant indebtedness. Barnett (1978) told of an interview with a Terminal Island prisoner who resorted to fraudulent activity because of pressures caused by speculation in the commodities market. In relating what happened to him, the inmate stated: "When we were first in business, we covered (bought a futures contract to hedge the risk) every coffee option we sold, then we covered half, then 10 percent, and then one day we sold more coffee options than could possibly have been covered by all the commodities exchanges in the world. There was no place we could go to buy all those coffee futures contracts, so we just ran it like an insurance company. We would lose a percentage, and we would pay our losses and our expenses with our winnings." This offender started out honestly without intending to break the law, but got caught up in the business excitement, over-extended himself, and got backed into a corner. With his back against the wall, he felt he had no other alternative but to commit fraud.

In some cases, company officials manipulated the price of their own companys' stock for personal or corporate benefit. One example of this phenomenon is the Westec case. In 1964, Carl M. was the president of a small company with an annual net income of about $10,000. Over the next 18 months, he merged with 17 other companies under the name of Westec. In 1964, Westec's stock sold for $4.50 on the American Stock Exchange, and by April of 1966, it was selling for $67. The chief beneficiary of this was Carl M., who held more than 400,000 shares of Westec common stock. To help the stock prices rise, Carl M. and his brother-in-law bought and sold large shares of stock. This created the misleading appearance that the stock was actively trading, thereby influencing the price and inducing others to buy. With the help of an outsider, Westec officers joined in a conspiracy to sell Westec shares that had not been registered with the Securities & Exchange Commission.

In August of 1966, 160,000 shares were purchased by or in behalf of Carl M., without adequate arrangements being made to pay for them. When news of this action leaked out, Westec's stock dropped 16 points in 13 days. When the bill for the 160,000 shares wasn't paid, the American Stock Exchange suspended the trading of Westec's stock. Carl M. and other company officials received jail sentences, and the CPA firm involved was censured.

Another example is Harvey P., president and majority owner of Continental Vending. He also owned approximately 25 percent of Valley Commercial Corporation, an affiliate of Continental. During 1958-1962, Harvey P. borrowed money from Valley to finance his personal stock-market speculations. Valley, in turn, borrowed money from Continental. Although he intended to repay such loans by the end of each year, he owed nearly $3.5 million by September 1962. During the 1962 audit, he informed the auditors that he was unable to repay the $3.5 million to Valley, but agreed to post collateral. However, the collateral amounted to only $2.9 million, and 80 percent was stock in Continental Vending. By certification date, the receivable from Valley had increased to $3.9 million and the collateral had decreased $270,000 in market value. Once the financial statements were issued, the stock value fell $720,000. Two weeks later, the stock value dropped $2 million. In February of 1962, the SEC suspended trading of Continental Vending on the American Stock Exchange. Harvey P. pleaded guilty and was sentenced to 18 months in prison. Six high-level employees resigned during the ensuing five-month period. Three of Continental's auditors were fined after being convicted of mail fraud, violation of the 1934 SEC Act, and filing false statements with a governmental agency.

Another example of fraud that was perpetrated to cover stock market speculation was the case of the P. T. Clark Company, a broker dealer firm. According to one office, "the firm's downfall came after it sold short millions of dollars in 'borrowed' securities, then couldn't deliver the stock when the price declines it expected didn't occur" (WSJ, 1975b). The short sales involved several of the most volatile glamour stocks on the New York Stock Exchange. Because the losses left P. T. Clark without enough liquid capital to satisfy SEC requirements, it falsified its books and records.

What to do: The first four causes of situational pressure stem from poor financial management. The obvious solution to this problem is to avoid extensive debt and unwise expenditures. However, this is easier said than done. Managers generally do not know the financial condition of employees. Even if they knew that some employees were over-extended, they would probably feel reluctant to talk about it with them. Furthermore, most employees think their financial problems are none of their employer's business.

Employers can do several things to reduce situational pressures caused by financial problems. However, they must be done with good judgment. The solution consists of two actions: discovering when an employee is having financial difficulty and doing something about it. Sometimes it is not too difficult to know if employees have financial troubles because rumors travel rapidly. Unfortunately, the kinds of pressures that contribute to fraud are the non-sharable problems. These pressures are not as likely to enter the rumor grapevine. The best approach, therefore, is to create a climate of openness and trust, where employees and managers feel free to confide in each other. The following ideas ought to be considered.

• Give special attention to employees whose wages are garnished. Provide financial counseling if they are interested.

• Provide a cash advance for employees who have short-term emergencies. A cash advance is a legal solution to a pressing financial need, and it also identifies who is having difficulties. Some organizations have a policy of loaning employees one month's salary, interest free, and spreading the repayments over the next 12 months. This arrangement is only intended for emergencies. It gives employees the feeling that there is somewhere acceptable and legal to turn to in times of financial trouble. Special counseling and encouragement can be provided for employees who need to borrow money. Curtis (1960) said that employers should give special attention to employees who have excessive charges, garnishment of their salaries, are borrowing heavily, or show any unusual signs of financial weakness.

• Provide financial information about loans. Occasionally employees do not know that money is available through loans. Money is often available at special rates to help specific individuals in buying a home, getting an education or furthering their training, but employees are not aware of these opportunities.

• Provide adequate expense accounts. If employees are expected to work with business associates who have expensive life-styles, they should have expense accounts that allow them to do so comfortably.

• Occasionally put the company on a "diet" when the style of living gets too plush. Employees tend to pattern their own life-styles at home after the life-style they see at work. Lavishly furnished offices, generous expense accounts, and expensive living at work create an appetite for conspicuous consumption at home. The work place contributes to the reasons why many people live beyond their means. To reduce this pressure, a company could occasionally conduct an austerity program: turning off lights, reducing the amount of travel, counting the number of pages copied, reducing telephone budgets, and other such measures.

• Provide financial advice about investing in the stock, bonds, and commodities markets. People should be encouraged to follow sound principles of personal investment.

EXCESSIVE GAMBLING

One of the oldest explanations for fraud is that it is motivated by illegal, immoral, or socially unapproved activities. Several authors list gambling as one of these activities (Nettler,

1974; Geis, 1968; Curtis, 1960; and U.S. Chamber of Commerce Handbook, 1974). Lillian (1968) stated that surety companies estimate between 30 and 75 percent of fraud losses are due to gambling. Quinney (1964) stated that risk-taking tendencies, especially gambling in business ventures, often lead to fraud. Russell (1975) gave an example of an employee with 30 years tenure who had acquired two vices, a fondness for gambling and for liquor. He made the mistake of placing his bets with underworld bookmakers, and when he couldn't cover his debts, fear drove him to embezzling company funds and cashing bad checks.

A gambler's fate goes up and down. When it is down, it can create strong pressures to commit fraud to cover the losses. Obtaining money illegally is especially likely when the gambler is going for high stakes or does so often. A recent example of this phenomenon is the REA Express Company, once a big name in the freight business. In the last years of its existence, its officers supposedly stole over $1 million from the company. Of the lost money, at least part of it went to support one officer's hobby of betting on and breeding horses (WSJ, 1978).

Another example of this phenomenon is Robert S., chief teller of a large savings bank in New York. Over a period of three years, he embezzled $1.5 million. Robert S. took his first $5,000 right after an audit, and later stated that he only intended to borrow the money to bet it at the races and then replace the original $5,000. He lost $3,000 the first night and the remaining $2,000 the second night. He stated that until he was caught, his gambling was an attempt to win back and replace the original $5,000 and all subsequent losses. He remained undetected for three years. When the F.B.I. raided a bookie joint, they noticed that he was betting up to $30,000 a day. Upon investigation, they thought it was inconsistent for someone to bet $30,000 a day when he only earned $11,000 a year. He then confessed to defrauding the bank to feed his compulsive gambling habit.

As examples of the kind of pressure gambling places on people, consider the following excerpts from the diaries of reformed gamblers (*U.S. News and World Report,* 1980):

(1) *Terry A.:* "When I was at the blackjack table, my wife could have been home dying from cancer, and I could not have cared less."

(2) *Phil T.:* "When I caught that first whiff of the race track, I was king in my own fantasy world. There is no other high like it."

(3) *Marge W.:* "I stole vacation money from the family sugar jar. I spent every waking hour thinking about getting to the track."

(4) *Thomas J.:* "Gambling was the ultimate experience for me—better than sex, better than any drug. I had withdrawal tortures just like a heroin junkie."

(5) *Ronald P.:* "I degraded myself in every way possible. I embezzled from my own company; I conned my 6-year-old out of his allowance."

(6) *Archie K.:* "After I woke up from an appendectomy, I sneaked out of the hospital, cashed a bogus check, and headed for my bookie. I was still bleeding from the operation."

(7) *Irving J.:* "I'll never forget coming home from work at night, looking at my family waiting for me, and then leaving to place a couple more bets. I was crying the whole time, but I had simply lost all control."

INVOLVEMENT WITH MEMBERS OF THE OPPOSITE SEX

One of the most popular theories explaining fraud is often referred to as the unholy trinity of babes, booze, and bets (Nettler, 1974; Freedman, 1973; Curtis, 1960; Chamber of Commerce Handbook, 1974; Lillian, 1968; Kintzele and Kintzele, 1976). Leven's (1964) study of 100 fraud perpetrators showed that 41 percent of those in financial difficulty stated that their troubles were caused by heavy social expenditures. One individual who had embezzled hundreds of thousands of dollars from his church, had with him upon entering prison, a picture of himself taken in Las Vegas with his arms around two beautiful blondes standing behind a table loaded with booze. Another officer (of the now defunct REA Express Company) said he spent his ill-gotten funds on a new car, wine, women, and song (WSJ, 1978a).

EXCESSIVE USE OF ALCOHOL OR DRUGS

It is difficult for most people to support an alcohol or drug habit on their regular salaries, so funds to support those habits often have to be obtained dishonestly. A number of authors have stated that alcohol is a contributor to fraud (Jefferey, 1970; Nettler, 1974; U.S. Chamber of Commerce, 1974; and Curtis, 1960). Reimer (1941) found that alcoholism was a factor in 18 of his 100 embezzlement cases. A study of 97 offenders by Levens (1964) showed that nine percent indicated their financial troubles were caused by drinking. Both Robert S. (Union Dime Savings Bank) and Mark P. (REA Express) partially attributed their actions to problems caused by drinking. Perhaps the most impressive evidence of a relationship between dishonesty and substance abuse is the research of Terris and Jones (Terris, 1979; Jones, 1980). They surveyed a large sample of employees and reported a positive relationship between dishonesty and substance abuse, that is, drug use and alcoholism.

What to do: Employers may be reluctant to do much about alcoholism, drug use, gambling, and sexual involvements. Even though an empirical relationship has been demonstrated between fraud and drug use, many drug users do not commit fraud. Inquiries about these issues may be seen as an invasion of one's personal privacy, and efforts to influence an individual's behavior may be considered an intrusion into one's personal life.

Nevertheless, gambling, prostitution, and substance abuse are expensive appetites that usually create enormous situational pressures. Furthermore, they are generally considered immoral and/or illegal by society. Employers may want to initiate some effort to reduce these problems not only to reduce fraud, but also to allow these people to become better employees. The following ideas are suggested for consideration.

• Alcoholism is an emotional and physical illness requiring

professional assistance. Suggestions to alcoholics that they cut down on their drinking are almost totally ineffective. Ignoring the problem only allows it to get worse. Alcoholics need to be confronted with the reality of the situation: that their performance is inadequate (it usually is), and they have the option of being fired or accepting professional help. Most alcoholics have a tendency to rationalize endlessly.

• People who drink socially can be encouraged to cut down on their drinking. If they realize that their drinking is physically harmful, destructive to their work performance, and very expensive, they are inclined to reduce their drinking.

• Drug addiction involves both a physical and a psychological dependence on drugs. Drug addicts need professional assistance to help them "dry out."

• Compulsive gambling is a disorder that should be treated with personal counseling.

• The personal behavior of employees is influenced by the expectations of managers and the social climate in the company. Three martini lunches, social hours, and office celebrations with alcoholic beverages create a climate that contributes to alcoholism. Likewise, gambling and involvement with the opposite sex are fostered by suggestive company parties, conventions at casinos, and extensive out-of-town travel. While the company cannot legislate or police individual morality, it can exert a lot of subtle pressure by the type of environment it creates and the expectations that are communicated.

UNDUE FAMILY, COMMUNITY, OR SOCIAL EXPECTATIONS

Sometimes the most intense pressure is not financial but psychological. Psychological pressure can't be measured and usually can't be completely removed. Social pressures from family and community expectations can be intense, endless, and self-imposed. Lottier (1942) has stated that everyone has a price, although the price may be social rather than monetary. LaPiere and Farnsworth (1949) stated that an individual is often faced with the alternative of committing fraud or losing something he values above his integrity. The item of value can take many different forms, including marriage, family, reputation, company position, career, or community standing

(Cressey, 1954; U.S. Chamber of Commerce, 1974; Lillian, 1968). Spencer (1965) stated that the typical perpetrator is pushing for upward mobility. His parents usually came from a considerably lower class than his present status, he generally has less education than others in the same occupation, and he belongs to social and civic clubs to help his upward climb. Mannerheim (1965) studied 30 English offenders and found essentially the same result: that the prisoners' striving for upward mobility led them into fraudulent activities. Quinney (1963) found that perpetrators were more likely to have had mothers who had high expectations of them. The perpetrator has sometimes depended upon a person of great moral strength to guide and direct his life. In studying a group of offenders, Reimer (1941) found that preceding the crime, the offender often lost the person who was acting as his conscience. Reimer (1941) labeled these social situations and pressures "the social push."

PERCEIVED INEQUITIES IN THE ORGANIZATION

Another form of situational pressure contributing to fraud is the perceived inequities within the organization. Most situational pressures contributing to fraud are direct financial pressures, where individuals have an acute, immediate need for money. Perceived inequities in the organization, however, are indirectly associated with money. If an employee is passed over for a promotion, he might embezzle out of a feeling of revenge. The pressure is not to have the money, but rather to satisfy a feeling of being "wronged." This desire to satisfy a feeling of injustice has been mentioned frequently as an explanation for fraud. In fact, a frequent observation has been made that fraud occurs most often when there is motive beyond money that encourages or justifies the criminal act. If an individual feels wronged, it is easy to rationalize the fraud as compensation for the injustice. Some of the most frequently-mentioned reasons for employees to "correct" past wrongs by committing fraud include (a) being passed over for promotion; (b) being assigned to undesirable jobs; (c) being subjected to severe disciplinary actions; (d) feeling that wage increases are inadequate; (e) seeing indications of favoritism toward other employees; (f) feeling resentment toward supervisors or authority figures in general; and (g) feeling frustrated on the job (Carson, 1977; Cressey, 1950; Hernon, 1976; Zeitlin, 1971; Jefferey, 1970; U.S. Chamber of Commerce, 1974; Lillian, 1968; and Gottheimer, 1978).

Russell (1975) gives an example of a long-time employee who had compiled a good record and was passed over for a raise that he felt he had earned. He was earning $15,000 a year and decided that he was entitled to a 10 percent raise. He therefore stole $125 a month, which was exactly 10 percent of his salary. His moral standards permitted him to steal that much because he felt it was his due, but he could not embezzle one cent more since it would have been dishonest.

Resentment toward a supervisor may or may not be justified by the supervisor's behavior. Nevertheless, feelings of hatred toward a supervisor, legitimate or not, can encourage an employee to commit a criminal act. The Chamber of Commerce (1974) stated that a deep-seated feeling of not being appreciated by a supervisor, or the resentment of superiors could lead to fraud. Curtis (1960) stated that some people steal because they are hostile towards their employers; they erase their guilt by thinking of examples of supervisory unfairness. DiTullio (1969) indicated that he found perpetrators to have an insufficient capacity for criticism. Therefore, they would most likely resent the supervisor even when the criticism was called for. Pecar (1975) made the conjecture that some criminal offenses are related to a disturbance in attitude toward authority and an underdeveloped sense of ownership of socially-owned property. Jaspan (1974) mentioned that a feeling of being unfairly treated by a company can lead to sabotage and fraud. Gottheimer (1978) told of a case where disenchantment with top management led an individual into fraudulent activity. In this case, the chief accountant of a large California produce-growing company developed a computer program to falsify and systematically raise all the company's monthly production costs by tiny increments. The extra monies were siphoned off into accounts of dummy customers, then pocketed by the accountant. When finally apprehended, the perpetrator expressed a lot of resentment toward top management, but felt very little remorse for the crime.

Pressure can also occur because of frustrations in performing a job. The frustrations may or may not be a normal part of the job, and there might not be any rational reason why the frustration should lead to fraud, but fraud might occur anyway. Klein and Densmore (1977) stated that if an employee feels inadequate or is frustrated in his attempts to handle his own responsibilities, he has the alternative of either failing or resorting to fraud in order to accomplish his goals or to meeting the employer's standards. They also stated that a bored employee may embezzle to make the job more exciting. Low morale, caused by severe disciplinary actions, substandard working conditions, or unfair or inconsistent policies, can also lead to frustration and thereby contribute to fraud. Leibholz (1974) even states that a lack of adequate ability or skill can lead to fraudulent activities because of the frustration the individual chooses to express through criminal actions.

CORPORATE OR PEER-GROUP PRESSURES

Employees often experience pressure to achieve performance goals in their work. This pressure can be very overwhelming at times, especially for managers. The source of the pressure can come from the individual's own aspiration levels, or it can come from the performance goals of higher-level executives. Baumhart (1961) administered an extensive questionnaire to businessmen and concluded that a person's colleagues in a company have a strong influence on the person's behavior. This finding was supported by a more recent study done by Carroll (1975), who investigated managerial ethics. In his survey, Carroll asked managers to indicate their attitudes about business ethics by agreeing or disagreeing with various statements. The first statement was: "Managers today feel under pressure to compromise personal standards to achieve company goals." Almost 65 percent of the managers agreed with the statement. This feeling was particularly prevalent at the middle and lower levels of management (84 percent agreement). Another statement was: "I can perceive of a situation where there are sound ethics running from top to bottom, but because of pressures from the top to achieve results, the person down the line compromises." Approximately 78 percent of the managers agreed with this statement. A third statement said: "The junior members of Nixon's reelection committee who confessed that they went along with their bosses to show their loyalty is just what young managers would have done in business." Almost 60 percent of the respondents agreed that this was, in fact, the case. It is interesting to note that 63 percent of the top managers disagreed with this assertion, whereas 61 percent of the middle managers and 85 percent of the lower managers agreed. This indicated the real possibility that top management can inadvertently be insulated from organizational reality with respect to particular issues. The significant finding of this study was that managers, particularly those below the top level, feel pressures to conform to what they perceive a superior's expectations of them to be, even though it requires them to compromise their personal values and standards (Carroll, 1975; DeMarco, 1978). These pressures could easily cause one to become involved in fraudulent activity in order to meet the expectations of superiors.

The *Wall Street Journal* (1979a), contained an article on how some middle managers cut corners to achieve high corporate goals. They said that when properly applied, either through the threat of punishment or the promise of reward, pressure can motivate employees to turn in their maximum performance. Sometimes, though, corporate goals are set too high or are simply unreasonable. Then an employee often confronts a hard choice; either to risk being labeled incompetent by telling superiors that they ask too much, or to begin taking unethical or illegal short cuts. When a manager feels his job or his division's survival is at stake, the corporation's standards of business conduct are apt to be sacrificed.

An example is an incident at one of Dorsey Corporation's glass-container plants. The plant manager, aware that the aging facility's output was falling behind that of other company plants, began to fear that Dorsey would close his plant and throw him and 300 other employees out of work. According to the company, the plant manager secretly started altering records and eventually inflated the value of the plant's production by about 33 percent. The over-reporting was discovered when a janitor, ignoring the manager's order to burn the actual records, instead hid the documents behind a chicken coop and showed them to company auditors visiting on an inspection tour.

Another example is the H. J. Heinz Co. A former official at the plant indicated that when employees didn't meet managements' growth targets, the top brass really came down on them. Everybody knew that if you missed the targets often enough, you were out on your ear. In this environment, some harried managers apparently resorted to deceptive bookkeeping when they couldn't otherwise meet profit goals set by the company's top executives. Invoices were misdated and payments to suppliers were made in advance, sometimes to be returned later in cash, all with the aim, insiders say, of showing the sort of smooth profit growth that would please top management and impress securities analysts.

Often individuals become aware of fraudulent activities, but fail to report them because they don't want to get involved. Jaspan (1972) indicated that many executives, including department heads and supervisors, may be aware of improper practices, but do nothing about them in order to avoid distasteful situations. They are afraid of losing friendships or being found at fault and criticized, or they may be intimidated by the fear of social rejection, bodily harm, or the loss of their jobs. Russell (1975) indicated that the passive acquiescence of those who don't want to get involved, or who find it repugnant to disclose dishonesty by fellow workers, is a growing factor in the failure of the separation of duties to prevent fraud. Employees who know that fellow workers are getting away with something may feel that someone in authority is protecting the illicit operation, or else it would not be allowed to continue. Also, self-preservation can be a powerful argument in "minding one's own business."

An employee of Equity Funding was asked what he would do if, when he began his career with the company, he had known what the company was doing. He was quoted as saying, "I guess I would have quit or else done just what I did and not get involved." He hesitated, then said, "I am not a hero; I don't know any heroes, do you? You just do your job."

What to do: If social pressures cause fraud, the apparent solution is to eliminate the pressures. Again, however, the apparent solution is not so easy, and in many respects it's wrong. All pressures cannot and should not be eliminated. Pressure to achieve social and community expectations provides a powerful source of motivation for individuals. Achieving organizational goals is also a source of tremendous satisfaction. Frustration in performing a job ought to be reduced, but all frustrations cannot be removed. Some jobs simply can't be enriched or automated out of existence.

Managers should try to reduce unnecessary pressure and frustrations and provide safety valves when pressures mount. The management literature is filled with suggestions for eliminating the pressures, resentments, and injustices that employees feel. The following suggestions are typical.

- Career counseling should assess an employee's long-term aspirations and provide a realistic concept of how the employee might expect to advance in the future. If employees discover that their expectations are unrealistic, they can either change their expectations or find other jobs more consistent with their expectations.

- Develop a communication system for employee complaints. In most unionized companies, a formal grievance procedure exists through which employees can express themselves if they feel mistreated. Other companies also need a process for expressing complaints. Some companies use a suggestion box that receives both suggestions and complaints. Other companies have formal surveys in which the employees complete an anonymous questionnaire assessing the organizational climate and their jobs.

- Have employees participate in setting their own performance goals and avoid placing excessive rewards and punishments on the employees' success or failure. When employees participate in setting their own goals, they feel a stronger commitment to reach them because they "own" them. Their motivation is internal, and they are more likely to achieve what they have committed themselves to. Furthermore, the goals will probably be more realistic. The tendency to make false performance reports or to use illegal means to achieve the goals results largely from the kinds of rewards or punishments offered. The pressure increases as the potential reward or punishment increases.

VALIDATION OF THE SITUATIONAL PRESSURE RED FLAGS

As shown above, there are several situational pressures that can contribute to fraud. These factors were identified by many authors having diverse backgrounds. In order to validate these red flags, we examined the literature (news articles, documentaries, etc.) on 52 past cases of fraud to see if these pressures were associated with the cases. The results, which are summarized in Table 4 of Appendix D, show that all 10 pressures were represented in the cases.

✳ SUMMARY POINTS OF CHAPTER 7 ✳

* Fraud can be perpetrated by:
  1) an individual against the company for personal benefit, or
  2) by management on behalf of the company.
* Excessive personal needs or pressures contribute to reasons why individuals commit fraud.
* It is important to tune into the language and justifications of the fraud perpetrator, such as "borrow," "temporary," "I had no choice," or "it isn't illegal."
* Evidence of situational stress may initially need to be inferred from comments made by individuals about themselves or others. Statements indicating indebtedness, insufficient means, excessive external or internal expectations, frustrations, expensive habits, or excessive ambition should be investigated.
* Personal financial factors that can lead to fraud are:
  1) high personal debts
  2) significant personal losses
  3) inadequate income
  4) living beyond one's means.
* Personal habits that can lead to fraud are:
  1) extensive stock market or other types of speculation
  2) extensive gambling
  3) illicit involvement with members of the opposite sex
  4) heavy use of alcohol or drugs.
* Personal feelings that can lead to fraud are:
  1) extreme community or social expectations to succeed
  2) perception of being treated unfairly or inadequately by the organization
  3) resentment of superiors
  4) frustration with the job
  5) peer-group pressures within the company
  6) unsatiable desire for self-enrichment or personal gain.

8

HOW TO REDUCE
FRAUD
OPPORTUNITIES

Chapter 8 Explains:

- How opportunities contribute to fraud.
- What opportunities are created by individuals.
- What opportunities are created by organizations.
- How opportunities to commit fraud can be reduced.

Opportunity is the second explanation for fraud. Like situational pressures, however, convenient opportunities do not necessarily cause fraud, and there is no reason why they should. Individuals can choose to behave honestly if they want to, and some people successfully resist temptations to commit fraud in spite of the opportunity.

In general, however, the probability of fraud increases as the opportunities become more convenient. The occurrence of fraud is much more likely if the crime only requires a simple act, if the chances of being detected and caught are very small, or if the punishment is very light. On the other hand, fraud is not as likely if tight security and sound internal controls require an elaborate scheme to subvert them, if the likelihood of detection is high, and if the punishment is severe.

Unfortunately, it appears that opportunities to commit fraud are increasing, and the evidence (reviewed in Chapter 2 and described more fully in the Appendices) indicates that almost no one can be considered completely honest. Almost any individual who is placed in the right circumstance, with enough situational pressure and sufficient opportunity, is likely to commit fraud. Jaspan (1972) highlighted this by stating that bonding company statistics show that approximately 50 percent of all dishonest employees and fraud perpetrators are too weak to withstand the bad example of others.

Fraud would not be committed unless there was an available opportunity. In some instances the opportunity has been created by careless organizational practices. In others, individuals create their own opportunities. Thus, numerous researchers have noted the importance of reducing opportunities to defraud as a necessary step in reducing fraud. Klein and Densmore (1977) suggested that the most important factor in fraud is the "opportunity" to commit it; that is, many employees would not steal or commit fraud if it were not so easy. Their conclusion was that since approximately 40 percent of all employees would not defraud if reasonable safeguards were present, management could eliminate a significant portion of all frauds by eliminating opportunities for dishonest actions.

Comer (1977) stated that for fraud to occur there must be an economic or psychological need, a moral justification, and an opportunity where the chances of detection are low. We agree with Reimer (1941) that any time an opportunity presents itself, in which the financial gains outweigh the risks involved, the probability of fraud increases significantly. Nettler (1974) suggested that embezzlement takes place when there is a meeting of desire and opportunity.

This chapter describes many factors contributing to opportunities to defraud, including some unique factors that may seem unusual. We believe that a careful analysis of fraud opportunities should include all attributes and policies of firms that not only make opportunities available, but also directly or indirectly encourage employees to seek these opportunities. Thus, opportunity also includes those factors which decrease the probability of a fraud being disclosed, and/or the perpetrator punished.

The remainder of this chapter discusses the following opportunities:

1. Familiarity with operations (including cover-up capabilities) and a position of trust

2. Too much trust in key employees

3. Close association with suppliers and other key people

4. Failure to inform employees about company rules and discipline of fraud perpetrators

5. Lengthy tenure in key jobs

6. Failure to use adequate personnel screening policies when hiring new employees to fill positions of trust

7. Failure to maintain accurate personnel records of dishonest acts or disciplinary actions

8. Failure to require executive disclosures and examinations

9. Dishonest or unethical management

10. Dominant top management by one or two individuals

11. Continual operation under crisis conditions

12. Failure to pay attention to details

13. Impersonal relationships and poor morale

14. Lack of internal security

FAMILIARITY WITH OPERATIONS AND A POSITION OF TRUST

An excellent opportunity to commit fraud exists when a perpetrator is in a position of trust and is sufficiently familiar with the operations to perpetrate the fraud and devise a cover-up scheme. Rose (1975) noted, after examining several fraud perpetrators, that 29 percent of them were between the ages of 51 and 60, which is considerably older than most property offenders. He suggested that many frauds require expertise that can only be obtained through many years of experience or training. Of the 51 persons Rose studied, 36 had worked at the same type of business almost exclusively or had at least acquired a good background knowledge of the business. Reimer (1941) stated that in addition to the necessary knowledge and skill to commit the crime, a fraud perpetrator must also have the ability to conceal the act and the skill necessary to anticipate and counteract a discovery. In many fraud cases, the crime was committed by the chief executives themselves (e.g., the president of Continental Vending) who were not only in positions where they were very familiar with company operations, but also where they could directly conceal it.

In his widely accepted explanation of fraud, Don Cressey

(1953) said that embezzlers must be in positions of trust that they perceive as offering private solutions to their personal needs. Specifically, the positions of trust must provide the employees with opportunities to satisfy their financial needs through the opportunities for fraud that are provided them. The positions of trust often insulate the potential perpetrators from suspicion and make them feel that there is little probability of being caught. Curtis (1960) suggested that employees who are given the freedom to come to work early or stay late because of their position of trust are given added opportunity to defraud their company.

TOO MUCH TRUST IN KEY EMPLOYEES

Besides being placed in a position of trust, some employees are given too much trust. They are given the authority to make major financial decisions and commit large amounts of money without having to justify or defend their actions. Morgensen (1975) indicated that a possible reason employees violate trust is that, with business enterprises becoming increasingly complex, trusted employees are more likely to operate in isolated and/or specialized contexts separating them from other individuals and thus providing them with a greater opportunity to commit fraud. Robert S. indicated that Union Dime placed too much supervisory authority in one individual's hands. He was trusted too much, and there were insufficient controls or checks and balances on his activities. He stated that if they would have had one other supervisor with the same responsibility, he could not have defrauded the bank.

What to do: Occupying a position of trust and being a highly-trusted employee clearly provides a more convenient opportunity for an employee to commit a fraud. However, managers cannot eliminate all positions of trust as a means of reducing fraud. Furthermore, some individuals must be trusted to handle money. Some of the most important work of a company is performed by people in positions of trust, and the effectiveness of the company depends heavily on their reliable performance.

Managers should be constantly aware of the convenient opportunity that exists for people in positions of trust to commit fraud. These positions should only be filled with employees who are highly trustworthy. Frequent accountability should also be expected.

• Carefully select people of high personal integrity to fill positions of trust.

• Create clear and explicit expectations about acceptable behavior.

• Require more frequent and thorough accountability from persons in positions of trust through budgeting and performance reports. Create the expectation that all financial decisions will be checked for accuracy and appropriateness.

CLOSE ASSOCIATION WITH SUPPLIERS AND OTHER KEY PEOPLE

The opportunity to commit a fraud is especially convenient for employees who are required to associate with other organizations, especially with those of their competitors. Employees in purchasing and buying departments are also constantly faced with situations where an arm's-length business transaction can easily be violated.

Comer (1977) suggested that employees who either have financial interest in a competitor, or close social or personal relationships with competitors are likely candidates for fraud. Fraud perpetrated with such outside accomplices can be decreased by requiring segregation of duties in all sensitive areas of a business. In fact, Leibholz and Wilson (1974) suggested a magic number of three employees working in any sensitive area as being the optimum number to prevent cooperation with outside parties.

An example of how close association contributed to fraud is shown in the Stirling Homex case. It was discovered that the president had other business dealings with nearly all of the buyers of his land deals. Before going public, well over half of Homex's sales were to companies in which the president had investments. In addition, the selection of board members led to a tangled web of relationships (*Business Week*, 1972). The corrupting influence of business associations was also very apparent in the Salad Oil case, where there were several instances of underworld connections. Several underworld figures were said to have direct connections with De Angelis's partner in his Chicago companies. The organized crime associations were so extensive that the company was refused a fat-processing license by the Chicago police.

What to do: Frequent associations with suppliers, buyers, and other business agents cannot be eliminated, but business transactions can be conducted at an arms-length.

• Require that accurate records be kept of all transactions. Check these records carefully for irregularities, such as purchases without the benefit of competitive bids, the use of early delivery, or the quality of goods as reasons for not accepting the lowest bid.

• Carefully select people of high integrity to work as purchasers, buyers, and in other jobs requiring close association with business contacts.

• Develop a manual outlining the company's policies and procedures regarding the business associations of purchasers, buyers, sales representatives, and others. This manual should contain a clear statement of the buyer-vendor relationship.

FAILURE TO INFORM EMPLOYEES ABOUT RULES AND DISCIPLINE OF FRAUD PERPETRATORS

The opportunity to commit fraud is psychologically more convenient when employees believe fraud normally goes undetected and unprosecuted. However, most companies try to hide information about the fraud they uncover in order to avoid adverse publicity. Even the company's own employees are typically not informed. Most experts agree, however, that the threat of punishment is a deterrent to crime.

Stone (1978) suggested that a firm that does not have a rigorous policy of informing its employees about the rules and disciplinary actions pertaining to fraud is more susceptible to fraud than other firms. Hernon (1976) and Carson (1977) suggested that, at the time of employment, all employees should receive a verbal orientation in which standards of honesty are explicitly described. In fact, Carson (1977) said that all employees should be required to sign a statement in which they acknowledge an understanding of company policies and a willingness to abide by them. Carson contended that these orientations tend to deter dishonest acts by removing uncertainty regarding the legality or appropriateness of questionable practices, such as borrowing company materials or accepting favors from suppliers. It has also been suggested that each employee should receive a copy of the company's employee policies and procedures manual, and that it should contain a general code of ethics, a set of rules for honest conduct, and specific penalties for dishonesty (Liebholz and Wilson, 1974; Jaspan, 1974; and Parker, 1978). These recommendations are consistent with the idea that if a person's fear of punishment is increased the likelihood of fraud will decline. If the firm's punishment of fraudulent acts is not made obvious, the fear of adverse consequences is greatly lessened. At Equity Funding, many employees, including nonmanagement personnel, realized that fraudulent acts were not being punished, so they too started embezzling. Loeffler (1974), a trustee of Equity Funding, noted that there seemed to be little common restraint. Officers of one subsidiary were embezzling funds by claiming personal travel and business expenses and charging many kinds of personal expenses to the company on a regular basis during the last months of the fraud.

What to do: All employees should know the rules and standards required by the company. Everyone should also believe that individuals who violate the rules will be caught and punished. This information needs to be widely disseminated.

• Prepare clearly-stated company policies that describe acceptable behavior. These policies should especially cover issues that are uncertain or unclear, such as conflicts of interest and the acceptance of gifts.

• Prosecute individuals who commit fraud and publicize the cases. Usually it is not financially expedient to prosecute everyone caught for dishonesty, but if no one is ever prosecuted or if people *think* no one is ever prosecuted, the probability of fraud will increase. Enough dishonest employees must be prosecuted and their convictions made public to create the belief that fraud perpetrators will be caught and punished.

LENGTHY TENURE IN KEY JOBS

Another factor that can create opportunities for fraud is the absence of mandatory vacations, periodic rotations, or transfers of executives and other key personnel. Employees in key positions can commit a fraud and carefully conceal it if they have total control over certain operations. The ability to conceal a fraud indefinitely, however, is thwarted when an outsider is required to perform the job during a vacation period or as a result of job rotations and periodic transfers.

One of the most famous cases in which the absence of vacations and job rotations became important was that of a major savings bank (Steffen, 1974), in which Robert S., the chief teller, embezzled approximately $1.5 million. In commenting on the fraud, he said: "If a bank coupled a two-week vacation period with four weeks of rotation to another job function, embezzlement would be nearly impossible to cover up." He believed that annual vacations for executives and periodic transfers between job positions would greatly eliminate the possibility of fraudulent activities. Geis (1968) suggested that fraud perpetrators, because they perceive themselves as law-abiding citizens, often isolate themselves and commit the fraudulent activity by themselves. If this is true, mandatory vacations and/or rotations should help to detect any solo fraudulent activity that is taking place. Kintzele and Kintzele (1976) and the Chamber of Commerce (1974) suggested that the shunning of vacations or promotions should be viewed as a serious warning signal of corporate fraud.

What to do: Lengthy job tenure provides a more convenient opportunity to design and commit a fraud. The cover-up is also easier to guarantee if individuals have total control over the relevant functions. The apparent solution is to avoid lengthy job tenures, i.e., do not allow employees to stay in the same jobs for a long time or have total control over any important functions. This is not a very satisfactory solution, however, because lengthy job tenure usually means that the job is staffed by a trained expert. Organizations usually try to achieve lengthy job tenure.

The solution, therefore, is to encourage lengthy job tenure but require periodic changes that eliminate the degree of domination required to commit and conceal a fraud.

• All employees should be required to take an annual vacation, during which time their job functions are performed by others.

• Key employees can be rotated periodically or transferred

to different functions. This not only makes fraud less convenient, it also increases job training and facilitates manpower planning by preparing more widely-trained employees.

INADEQUATE PERSONNEL-SCREENING POLICIES

Some individuals have a history of fraud and embezzlement. They go from job to job, usually stealing small amounts. Because the amounts are small and the evidence not too strong, these individuals are fired but not prosecuted. They find another job and continue their pattern of stealing. One retail store fired an employee for dishonesty and later learned that she had been fired from at least six other jobs within the past three years because of stealing. A careful background check on this individual before she was hired would have indicated that she was a poor risk.

Carson (1977) suggested that job application forms completed by prospective employees should request specific information regarding their qualifications for the present job, plus information about their past employment. He was adamant in his belief that employees' statements of previous activities should be thoroughly investigated for accuracy. Leibholz and Wilson (1974) also recommended that other references, in addition to the ones listed by the applicant, should be thoroughly checked. One of the most effective ways to check employee backgrounds is to use an investigative agency (Romney and Albrecht, 1979). Background checks can be purchased from several companies specializing in this kind of service, e.g., Guardsmark, Burns, Pinkerton, and other good detective agencies. One of the largest investigative companies is the Retail Credit Co.

An example of a fraud perpetrated by an employee whose background had not been thoroughly checked is the case in which a controller defrauded his company of several million dollars. After investigating the fraud, it was discovered that the controller had been fired from three of his previous five jobs in the last eight years. He was discovered in the defrauded company when the president appeared on the premises one night and found a stranger working in the accounting area. The nocturnal stranger was a phantom controller actually doing the work of the corporate controller, who wasn't even trained in accounting.

The U.S. Department of Commerce, in *Crime in Service Industries* (1977), suggested that the best way to stop employee theft is to simply not hire those employees who are inclined to steal. What the employer must do is to set up a screening process that will weed out obvious security risks. Many experts believe that personnel screening is one of the most vital safeguards against the internal threat of fraud. Concerning personnel screening policies, the Department of Commerce gives some basic guidelines:

> "Always have applicants fill out a written application. Exercise caution when considering ex-convicts. Solicit references but keep in mind that those contacted will usually give favorable opinions. Always interview. Use psychological deterrents such as informing the applicant that your business routinely runs a security check on background or that fingerprints will be taken (and checked against regulatory agency files). Obtain credit bureau reports and investigate." (U.S. Chamber of Commerce, 1977, pp. 101-102.)

Robert S., of Union Dime, indicated that banks place an almost unshakable trust in their employees. He stated that he was not polygraphed when he was first employed by Union Dime and that the bank did not have a periodic polygraphing policy. If they had practiced such procedures, they would have prevented him from embezzling $1.5 million. McBride (Miller, 1973), chairman of the Bank Administration's Institute Bank Security Commission, suggested that banks not only conduct extensive pre-employment background investigations of all personnel, but also that they continue to scrutinize employees throughout their term of employment. In addition, he suggests that the banks should also be aware of employees' activities both on and off the job.

FAILURE TO MAINTAIN ACCURATE PERSONNEL RECORDS OF DISHONEST ACTS OR DISCIPLINARY ACTIONS

The failure to maintain accurate personnel records of dishonest acts or disciplinary actions for such things as alcoholism and/or drug use can create an atmosphere conducive to fraud.

Carson (1977) recommended that all acts of dishonesty be placed in an employee's personnel file regardless of whether or not he was dismissed. He also suggested that personnel information which would make an employee a prime suspect of fraud be maintained in personnel files. Examples of information that should be included in the files are such things as major purchases of luxury items, large investments in real estate or stocks, sizable winnings and losses in gambling, membership in fraternities, business clubs, social organizations, and charitable organizations, that can indicate whether or not an employee is living beyond his or her income. While we agree that this type of information can be helpful, extreme caution and discretion should be exercised in gathering the data so that personal feelings and privacy laws are not violated.

NO EXECUTIVE DISCLOSURES AND/OR EXAMINATIONS

An indirect method of detecting fraud is to observe the spending and investing patterns of employees. It is unlikely that an employee will embezzle a million dollars and still follow the same conservative spending habits as before. Even the most careful fraud perpetrator will probably begin to make major purchases, take extended vacations, or in some way start to spend the embezzled money. People seldom commit fraud to hide the money indefinitely in a secret account.

Carson (1977) suggested that executives be required to submit a full disclosure of their financial condition on an annual basis. He recommended that this information be checked and that any dramatic changes be carefully examined and questioned. This financial disclosure could be required of all key executives on an annual basis, although the information would not need to be made completely public as in the case of public officials. Some individuals might dislike being required to submit a statement of their financial conditions, but most key executives would probably think the request was appropriate considering their position of trust.

DISHONEST MANAGEMENT

Baumhart (1961) stated that if executives are honest, there will be few problems of dishonesty among the other employees. The U.S. Chamber of Commerce (1974) added that a key situation which seems to be valuable in predicting fraud is the "honesty atmosphere of a company," or the extent to which honesty is upheld and taught. If dishonesty is found in other areas of the company (e.g., bribes, payoffs, falsifying government reports), a climate of dishonesty is encouraged. Schuessler (Sutherland, 1973) said that social groups differ in the importance they attach to respect for the law, and that individuals will move toward or away from crime according to the cultural standards of their associates, especially their intimate ones. The valuable insight contained here is that social interactions and interpersonal influences do more to set the stage for fraud than personal characteristics. As reported previously, bonding company statistics show that 50 percent of all employees involved in fraud were unable to withstand the bad example of others around them. Coopers & Lybrand's red flag list (1977) warns that fraud and embezzlement have a high probability of occurring in companies directed by executives with records of malfeasance.

It seems logical that it would be easier for an individual working under someone who is dishonest to become involved in deceitful activity. The Chamber of Commerce (1974) suggested there is strong evidence supporting the contention that sound leadership methods constitute the most essential precondition for an adequate level of integrity within the firm. Employees tend to accept the values of their company superiors. Comer (1977) suggested that fraud is perpetrated and the incentive to commit fraud is created in a climate of "moral decay" that filters down from the top and permeates middle management. He stated that fraud is less likely to occur if the manager of the firm is efficient and inquiring. If a manager is constantly on the golf course or at the bar, or is weak and generally incompetent, the risks of fraud are high.

An example of the influence of dishonest management is found in the Cenco Corporation. During the period 1970-74, the company reported false profits of approximately $25 million by inflating inventory values. One operation's manager who pleaded guilty said he personally prepared records to inflate Cenco's inventory and profits because "I was told to do it, and I went along." (WSJ, 1979.)

What to do: A climate of honesty is difficult to establish for two reasons. First, executives feel uncomfortable proselytizing for honesty because they think it is not "cool" socially. Advocating honesty seems too much like preaching. Talking in favor of social values does not create the same degree of excitement and public appeal as attacking them. Even if they are highly committed to corporate responsibility and personal integrity, most executives prefer to assume that everyone accepts honesty rather than actively advocating it personally.

Second, efforts to create a climate of honesty sometimes result in trivial disputes about picky issues and minor concerns. Nevertheless, some of these small issues involve questionable practices that tend to destroy a climate of honesty, or at least provide individuals with sufficient evidence to justify their perceptions of dishonesty. These questionable practices usually concern small issues like using a copy machine for personal use, using the company phone for personal long-distance phone calls, and taking home office supplies for personal use. Although such items may be financially unimportant, they can still be psychologically significant.

• Periodically, managers need to unequivocally endorse the importance of honesty as a basic principle guiding the conduct of the company.

• Questionable practices need to be carefully examined and guidelines must be developed. Using the company phone to make personal long-distance calls might be acceptable during certain times or every so often. The guidelines may need to be very explicit in some areas, but in others they might only need to give general direction.

DOMINANT TOP MANAGEMENT

The opportunity to commit and conceal a fraud is greater if a company, a division, or a department is directed by an individual (or group of collaborating individuals) who is extremely powerful. When a dominant individual is able to direct and control an organization without being challenged or questioned, there is a greater opportunity for fraud.

Sneath (1975) said "Management may have as a common factor a person of overpowering influence controlling the operations of a company, dominating those around him, and attempting to impose his views even upon the auditor."

Kapnick (1975), Touche Ross (1974), and the U.S. Chamber of Commerce (1974) also listed a dominant top management as a possible clue to fraudulent activities. Clarence Kelley (1976), former director of the F.B.I., related the case of a west coast bank that was closed when bank examiners discovered a series of irregular loans made by the bank. The ensuing F.B.I. investigation revealed that the bank president, who ruled with an iron hand, had been systematically looting the bank by issuing over 500 loans, based on financial statements, to dozens of skeleton corporations that he controlled. The proceeds of approximately 74 of these loans were found to have been deposited directly into accounts other than those of the borrowers'. Further tracing of the loans led to the discovery of special accounts for which the named account holder had no record. Following the close of the bank, the Federal Deposit Insurance Corporation called this case the largest bank failure in the history of the United States, and stated that it might result in the FDIC's paying the depositors claims in excess of $450 million.

In another example, it was the president who was the dominant figure in the Equity Funding case. He was said to run his company like an old fashioned schoolmaster would run a one-room school house. Once, when an employee asked for a vacation, the president simply said, "You're going to stay." The employee said that "to anyone else, I'd say 'Kiss my A--' but the president had this presence."

What to do: No one should have so much power that their decisions and actions cannot be challenged and examined. Executives need to have the authority to act decisively and deviate from normal procedures when the circumstances warrant it, but they should still be questioned and required to defend their actions.

OPERATING UNDER CRISIS CONDITIONS

During times of crisis or pressure, there are additional opportunities to commit fraud. During such events as remodeling or retooling, or when a special project is being hurried for completion, the normal system of internal controls is often pushed aside. Signatures are obtained authorizing uncertain purchases. Reimbursements are made rapidly and with little documentation. Record keeping falls behind and cannot be reconstructed. Materials come and go rapidly and can be easily misplaced. No one is entirely sure who is doing what.

Both Kapnick (1976) and Touche Ross (1974) listed operating under crisis conditions as a clue or red flag to the possibility of fraud. Touche Ross stated that when the accounting and financial functions appear to be understaffed resulting in constant crisis conditions, auditors and managers should beware of fraud. In a personal interview, the controller of one of the General Motors divisions suggested that in his firm, fraud was most likely to occur when a special project that got priority over all other work was done on a crisis basis. He suggested that for these types of projects, the normal internal controls are usually overlooked, thus making it easier to perpetrate fraud.

What to do: Times of crisis and pressure can sometimes be eliminated, but not always. Through advance planning, however, many of the opportunities to defraud can be reduced. Additional assistance can be obtained for the accounting staff, and additional security guards can be hired temporarily. Record keeping might fall behind for a time, but instructions to keep receipts and other records might enable the records to be updated accurately later.

INADEQUATE ATTENTION TO DETAIL

Another form of opportunity to commit fraud is created by the carelessness of managers. If managers do not give adequate attention to the details of how the company functions, it is easier to commit fraud.

There are a lot of good reasons why managers might not want to become involved in the details of the company. The responsibilities at each managerial level often require a broader perspective than the detailed information that is relevant at lower levels. Consequently, managers often prefer to assume that the technical details were competently performed by lower level subordinates, and then only choose to work on the summary reports. If they continually display an attitude of disinterest in the details, subordinates have a greater opportunity to misrepresent and misplace without being detected.

What to do: It is not realistic for managers to always check everything thoroughly. However, periodic or random checks show a concern for accuracy and decrease the perceived opportunity to have fraud go undetected. Occasionally, managers should thoroughly check the reports they receive and observe the actions and performance of their subordinates.

IMPERSONAL RELATIONSHIPS AND POOR MORALE

The quality of social interaction within an organization influences the opportunity to commit fraud. On one hand, employees who are members of a cohesive group may join together to commit a fraud. This form of collusion requires close interpersonal relationships among the members of the group. This does not mean that all cohesive groups will form a secret agreement for fraudulent or deceitful purposes. But close interpersonal relationships make collusion more convenient.

On the other hand, there are more opportunities to commit fraud in a large, impersonal organization where its members do not know each other well. A large corporation in Chicago, for example, lost almost 100 typewriters shortly after changing to a new location. During working hours, two men removed the typewriters without being stopped. Everyone assumed they worked for the corporation and were simply doing their job by moving the equipment.

Another reason poor interpersonal relationships contribute to fraud is because of conflict and frustration. As noted in the last chapter, some individuals interpret frustration and conflict as excuses for committing a criminal act.

Impersonal relationships and poor morale were cited by Klein and Densmore (1977) as factors that often contribute to fraud. They suggested that embezzlement can be a truncated form of conflict resolution and, as such, can be predicted to occur increasingly within bureaucratic systems that ignore the realities of conflict. A study of convicted embezzlers found that a significant number of them had experienced some kind of non-sharable problem that could not be discussed with their colleagues before committing embezzlement. When a company solves conflicts as they arise, embezzlement decreases. Unless honest and open relationships exist, conflicts cannot be shared and channeled into useful outlets. The U.S. Chamber of Commerce (1974) indicated that fraud is more likely to exist in situations where superiors are not appreciative of their employees. Carson (1977) suggested that as the distance in interpersonal relationships increases, more dishonesty can be expected. Reimer (1941) suggested that overwork and nervous exhaustion may also make an employee indifferent to the possible consequences of his criminal behavior.

Stone (1978) suggested that an employee with low morale has a much higher probability of committing fraud than an employee with high morale. This factor was also suggested by Klein and Densmore (1977) when they stated that bored employees may embezzle to make their jobs more exciting or to relieve frustration. If there are poor interpersonal relationships, frustrated managers who are not succeeding or who feel unable to handle their responsibilities may turn to fraud. This is particularly true if a company gives a person a goal to achieve but does not give him the means to accomplish it. Feelings of inadequacy and failure often culminate in fraud. The U.S. Chamber of Commerce (1974) stated that employees are diverted from ethical behavior by various on-the-job irritations, low and inadequate wages and salaries, resentment against the employer for alleged, unfair, or inconsistent policies, severe disciplinary actions, substandard working conditions, or a deep-seated feeling of not being appreciated by their supervisors.

Related to a feeling of impersonal relations with co-workers is an impersonal relationship with the company. Many employees feel alienated in their work because their performance is never noticed. No one evaluates their performance or measures their productivity. The U.S. Department of Commerce suggested that the failure to evaluate employee performance can adversely affect morale:

> Management should regularly evaluate employee performance. Unrealistic performance standards can lead either to desperation and anger, resulting in dishonesty, or to "get even" attitudes. Management should regularly review salaries, wages, and benefits with key employees. In addition, management should establish a grievance procedure and give employees an outlet for disagreement and be receptive of all grievances submitted. (U.S. Chamber of Commerce, 1977, p. 103.)

Carson (1977) suggested that performance appraisals should be conducted on each individual because he felt that if a person knows that he or she will be evaluated he will have a greater sense of accountability.

Leibholz and Wilson (1974) stated that if there is not a good channel of internal communication that includes feedback and evaluation, fraud will be more likely to exist. They suggested that management reviews should evaluate technical performance and attitudes towards others and/or towards problems. Jaspan (1972) has indicated that a proven way of destroying the roots of dishonesty is to measure work output and evaluate employee performance regularly. He indicated that people want to know how they are progressing and how management rates their efforts. Supervisors should have the responsibility to communicate this information on a monthly or quarterly basis, either orally or in writing. The knowledge that everyone's work is constantly being appraised and under supervision deters wrongdoing. It also provides incentives and upgrades employee respect for management and supervision.

LACK OF INTERNAL SECURITY

The most prevalent opportunities for fraud have usually stemmed from inadequate internal security. Each organization should have a carefully-designed system of internal security. Numerous books and articles have been written on internal security systems. Carson (1977) suggested that an organization needs to have a competent and well-trained security department. He noted that in too many instances, security departments consist of incompetent production employees and others who have not been properly trained in security measures. Carson stated that the security chief should report directly to the top corporate officers. In addition, he suggested that every organization needs to conduct a security survey to examine the major weaknesses in their security systems.

Jaspan (1972) stated that in more than 40 years of helping management control offices and strengthen systems, he has concluded that fraud and dishonest acts are as contagious as the measles or mumps. Fortunately, however, they are as curable as those diseases, provided the correct and proper dosages of concerned perventative management is administered. To reduce fraud, employers must develop a total approach toward preventing dishonesty within their organizations. Each company needs a comprehensive security program engineered to protect corporate assets. A good internal security system should focus on six potential targets to prevent dishonesty:

1. The security of the company's perimeter and traffic patterns in and out
2. The various procedures governing the flow of materials
3. The storage patterns and protection of different materials
4. Internal and external lock-up procedures
5. An efficient and effective guard force
6. Protection of sensitive information within the corporation

VALIDATION OF INDIVIDUAL-OPPORTUNITY RED FLAGS

Fourteen opportunities to commit fraud were identified in this chapter. These opportunities were identified by several authors describing the causes of fraud. To estimate how important these opportunities were in contributing to fraud, an examination of 52 cases of fraud was made. Table 5 in Appendix D shows how frequently each factor was mentioned in the 52 cases.

* SUMMARY POINTS OF CHAPTER 8 *

* Many acts of fraud would not be committed if it weren't so easy; many frauds could be eliminated by reducing opportunities for dishonest acts.
* Opportunity includes all attributes or policies of a firm or individual that makes fraud possible or decreases the probability that fraud will be disclosed or punished.
* Personally-created opportunities that can make fraud easier are:
    1) familiarity with operations (including cover-up capabilities) and
    2) close association with suppliers and other key people.
* Firm characteristics that make it easier for an individual to commit fraud are:
    1) failure to inform employees about rules and disciplines of fraud perpetrators
    2) rapid turnover of key employees
    3) absence of mandatory vacations
    4) absence of periodic rotations or transfers of employees
    5) inadequate personnel screening policies for hiring new employees
    6) absence of explicit and uniform personnel policies
    7) failure to maintain accurate personnel records for disciplinary actions
    8) failure to require executive disclosures
    9) dishonest or unethical management
    10) dominant top management
    11) constantly operating under crisis conditions
    12) paying little attention to details
    13) impersonal relationships or poor morale
    14) lack of internal security.

9

HOW TO ASSESS
PERSONAL
INTEGRITY

Chapter 9 Explains:

- Personality Variables Associated with Fraud.
- Differences Between Fraud Perpetrators and Other Property Offenders.
- Problems of Personality Assessment.
- Methods of Assessing Employee Trust.

People who are dishonest should not be given the responsibility of managing a company's financial resources. Organizations need to select individuals with high personal integrity to occupy positions of trust. In fact, the likelihood of fraud would be even lower if every employee who was hired had high personal integrity. This recommendation raises two important questions: (a) do some people actually have above average personal integrity that prevents them from criminal fraud, and (b) how can you identify these people?

The identification of dishonest people is not a simple process. In the written descriptions of some fraud cases, the cause of fraud was attributed in part to "greedy" people. These greedy people were thought to have unusually strong desires for personal gain and self-enrichment. Their greedy natures caused them to behave dishonestly; their criminal actions were motivated by their greed and avarice. Two particular cases where fraud was attributed to greedy people include Equity Funding and Homestake Production (Weinstein, 1974; Weiss, 1974). Superficially, these cases seem to indicate that greedy people should not be placed in positions of trust.

While the people who commit fraud may appear to be greedy, it is difficult to predict in advance who will be greedy. We usually do not label someone "greedy" until after they have acted dishonestly. How do we know who has an unusually strong desire for wealth? Almost everyone has a desire for wealth and personal gain and there is nothing wrong with having these desires unless you behave dishonestly. Even if an employer knew that someone had a tremendous desire for wealth and riches, there is an additional problem of deciding whether this person should be denied a position of trust. Having a strong desire for wealth does not necessarily mean that the person will behave dishonestly to obtain it. Furthermore, how strong does the desire for wealth have to be before it is considered unusually strong?

Two major approaches have been used to identify likely fraud perpetrators. The first approach is to develop a personality profile describing the personality of a typical fraud perpetrator. This approach is commonly used in the mental health profession as a means of categorizing disorders and prescribing treatment. Criminal profiles have also been developed for major kinds of criminal behaviors such as aggravated assault, forcible rape, and petty theft. The following sections (and Appendices A and C) will show, however, that fraud perpetrators do not seem to fit a particular personality profile.

The second approach is to directly measure the person's integrity. Personality variables are disregarded here; only the degree of honesty and integrity are assessed. This approach appears to show the greatest promise in selecting individuals to occupy positions of trust.

PERSONALITY VARIABLES ASSOCIATED WITH FRAUD

A popular belief in our society is that people who break the law are career criminals who have dishonest and anti-social personalities. Many people think that criminals are individuals who went the wrong way in life and developed a criminal personality. This popular myth suggests that all criminals have similar personalities, so what we should do is identify the criminal type and use this information to reduce crime.

Several attempts to explain criminal behavior have been made by correlating personality test scores with delinquency or criminal behavior. Some of the most extensively examined tests for predicting delinquency and criminality include the Minnesota Multiphasic Personality Inventory (Hathaway and Monachesi, 1953), the California Personality Inventory (Gough, 1965; Gough and Peterson, 1952), and the Bipolar Psychological Inventory (used in our analysis in Appendix C). Projective personality tests have also been used to predict criminal or delinquent tendencies.

One of the best examples of using personality tests to identify criminality is the research of Gough (1960). He found that one scale on the California Personality Inventory consistently yielded a higher average score for normal subpopulations than for delinquent and criminal subpopulations. This scale was the Socialization Scale, which is thought to differentiate well-socialized individuals from others. Studies by Gough and others have found that this socialization scale produces lower scores for criminals (e.g., county jail inmates and federal prisoners) than for normal groups (e.g., college students and "best citizens" in high school). Therefore, criminals seem to be lacking in the kinds of social restraints and conventions that govern the behavior of normal individuals. However, dramatic personality differences common to all criminals have not been found.

Unfortunately, the popular belief about criminal personalities is not correct. All criminals do not fit a common description of a single criminal personality. Instead, there appears to be different personality profiles for different kinds of crimes.

Over the past three centuries, several attempts have been made to determine the general causes of criminality. Gibbons (1973) analyzed these general theories of criminality and classified them into (a) physiological, (b) psychological, and (c) sociological explanations of crime. A review of these three theories of criminality is contained in Appendix A. Gibbons concluded that no single theory can explain all the complex forms of crime. Instead, he has suggested that different forms of crime, which he called criminal careers, should be examined separately. Just as there are different diseases that cause different illnesses, so also there are different criminal careers that lead to different forms of crime. Someone who commits forcible rape, for example, has a different kind of personality from someone who commits grand larceny.

Attempts to identify the criminal careers of fraud perpetrators have not been generally successful. People who commit fraud seem to be a heterogeneous group in which no personality variables or background characteristics are commonly shared. Fraud perpetrators do not seem to have much in common with other criminals, nor do they seem to have much in common with each other.

Many have attested to the heterogeneous nature of the fraud perpetrator and the absence of single identifying traits. Reasons (1974) pointed out that fraud is democratic, being committed by all levels and all types of people. This would even argue against any social class limitations. Edelhertz (1970) added his assertion of difficulty in identifying the offender when he stated that characteristics of fraud must be found in its mode of operation and objectives, rather than in the nature of the offenders. Hooton (1939) found that his embezzler group was more nearly like law-abiding citizens than other offending groups.

A study by Glick and Newsom (1974) indicated that they were unable to identify embezzlers because they simply did not fit any of the stereotypes of criminals. On the surface, they often appeared like normal persons: sincere, likeable, sociable, etc. This is probably the reason they inspired confidence, could remain above suspicion, and could go undetected for so long.

Several researchers have concluded that fraud perpetrators are different from other criminals, but that they are not unique as a group (Geis, 1968). It was probably stated best by Nettler (1974) who said, "There is, then, no one road to the violation of a vocational financial trust; there are many." Jefferey (1970) commented: "However, in the final analysis, it has to be concluded that there is no such thing as a typical embezzler. The personal characteristics, the background, the job status, the motives and the economic position of embezzlers are as varied as humanity itself." Even with this pessimistic and common view, there should be a continuing, but more rigorous research effort to link personal characteristics or traits with fraudulent offenses.

Because of the lack of empirical research on fraud perpetrators as a separate criminal career, a study examining fraud perpetrators was conducted. A full report of the study and the findings are presented in Appendix C. A sample of prisoners convicted of fraud was compared with two other groups. One of the comparison groups was made up of prisoners convicted of property offenses. Both the property offenders and fraud perpetrators had been convicted for stealing, but fraud perpetrators were involved in a unique kind of stealing. The other comparison group was comprised of college students enrolled at a major university.

The results of this study help to explain why fraud perpetrators cannot be described by a criminal career profile. The findings indicated that incarcerated fraud perpetrators are more like the average population than like other criminals. Numerous differences between fraud perpetrators and other property offenders were observed in both their background characteristics and their personality variables. In comparing incarcerated fraud perpetrators with other property offenders, it was found that they:

1. Included a higher percentage of women
2. Were more likely to be married
3. Were less likely to be divorced
4. Were less likely to have used drugs
5. Were less likely to have used alcohol
6. Were less likely to be tattooed
7. Were more likely to be church members
8. Were less likely to have no religious preference
9. Were less likely to have been in a juvenile institution
10. Were less likely to have escaped from prison or jail
11. Were less likely to have run away from a juvenile institution
12. Were less likely to have been on probation
13. Were older
14. Were heavier
15. Had more children
16. Had completed more grades in school
17. Had been arrested fewer times
18. Were first arrested at an older age
19. Took more valid tests, i.e., had greater consistency in their test answers

20. Were more optimistic
21. Had higher self-esteem
22. Were more self-sufficient
23. Were more achieving
24. Had more family harmony
25. Were more socially conforming
26. Had more self-control
27. Were more kind
28. Were more empathetic

Each of the above differences were statistically significant. When considered in total, the results indicate that fraud perpetrators are quite different from other property offenders. In general, the fraud perpetrators had more healthy, stable personalities and more socially acceptable background characteristics.

The personality comparisons between the fraud perpetrators and the college students also supported the idea that fraud perpetrators are generally quite normal. When the fraud perpetrators were compared with a sample of college students, the comparisons indicated that the two groups were quite similar on nine traits. Only on the following six traits were there significant differences. Fraud perpetrators:

1. Were more dishonest
2. Had more psychic pain
3. Were more independent
4. Were more sexually mature
5. Were more socially deviant
6. Were more empathetic

The results of this study support the conclusion that fraud perpetrators are not "common" criminals. These results were consistent with the observations of many prison officials who have said, "White-collar criminals are quite different from the rest. They are more like us than they are like the other criminals."

PROBLEMS IN IDENTIFYING THE PERSONALITIES
OF FRAUD PERPETRATORS

An examination of the literature on fraud reveals little empirical data concerning personality traits that would identify or set apart those individuals who engage in fraudulent acts. The paucity of research findings on personality traits for this group is not entirely unexpected. There are many reasons for the lack of good research.

Very few organizations give personality tests to their employees. So, even when they have a large sample of former employees who have been terminated for dishonesty, the organizations are not able to develop a good profile of the fraud perpetrators.

Fraud perpetrators are not part of a homogenous group. For example, the offender may be an employee, a top executive, or even a corporate entity. There is little agreement among criminologists about basic definitions of the phenomenon, or how to classify the persons involved.

Social class is not a distinguishing factor. The nature of the crime is usually occupationally related, but variations range from minor misappropriation of funds to major stock or land frauds perpetrated by a group.

Unlike other criminal groups, fraud offenders are seldom available to be studied as a group. Incarcerations are not routine, probation is more likely, and simply being dismissed from the company is even more probable as punishment. In fact, most fraud perpetrators are probably not even caught. Even prosecutions that are started are often discontinued. Overall, there is a tendency to dismiss, smooth over, and forget the offense as soon as possible, primarily to avoid adverse publicity by the victimized company. Therefore, the individuals are not available to be studied.

Finally, researchers are not able to contrive a laboratory situation that provides the necessary conditions for a study of the causes of fraud. Such an experiment would require: a controlled experimental situation that appeared real to the subject; the ability to systematically alter the situation to investigate various causes; and a sample of managers who could be observed in different situations.

Since they are part of such a heterogeneous group, fraud perpetrators would probably not evidence many common characteristics predictive of their crime, even if the above problems were overcome. Subgroupings into more homogeneous groups could possibly yield different types of fraud perpetrators who could then be described and differentiated from one another. To our knowledge, this has not yet been done systematically.

In summary, the assumption that all fraud perpetrators have something in common is probably false (aside from a broad, general definition of their crime). Therefore, the absence of personal characteristics that set fraud perpetrators, as a group, apart from other people is not proof that personality variables are irrelevant. Personal factors might be useful in describing fraud perpetrators if they are subdivided into homogeneous units and researched. For example, some retail companies have developed a profile of the typical employee who takes money from a cash register. The profile indicates that they tend to be young and new to the company, but do not have especially unique personalities.

MORAL DEVELOPMENT

While empirical research has not focused specifically on fraud, numerous experiments have examined honesty and other moral behaviors. These studies provide considerable insight into the causes of fraud and give evidence for the recommendations presented in this book.

As noted in Chapter Two, management fraud, embezzlement, kickbacks, bribes, and theft are all forms of dishonest behavior. When an executive misrepresents a business transaction or steals from the company, he is behaving dishonestly. When a computer technician manipulates the computer system to place the fraction of a cent from each employee's payroll calculation into a hidden account that he can withdraw from, he is behaving dishonestly. When a purchasing agent receives kickbacks by arranging to make purchase orders and payments for more merchandise than is received, he is behaving dishonestly.

Honesty is a "moral" behavior. Moral behaviors consist of those actions that are considered intrinsically desirable, valued, and good because of their contribution to the betterment of society. Most of the research on moral development has focused on three "moral" behaviors: honesty, aggression, and pro-social behaviors. Theories of moral development help explain why some people behave honestly while others do not.

The early researchers on honesty expected to find that it was a stable personality variable—honest people would always try to act honestly and dishonest people would always try to cheat. The initial research, however, did not confirm this expectation. An extensive research study done on over 8,000 youths from 1924-1930, concluded that honesty was not a general, personal trait in the same way that intelligence and achievement were general traits (Hartshorne and May, 1928). This study found that honest or dishonest behavior in one situation was not necessarily related to behavior in a different situation. Students who cheated in one activity did not necessarily cheat in other activities. The study concluded that honesty and dishonesty were determined by the situation (e.g., the importance of succeeding and the chances of being caught), rather than from a general personality trait.

Later research (Burton, 1963) has confirmed that honesty is situationally determined, but only for some people. Others develop a general trait of honesty or dishonesty. The difference between situational honesty and generalized honesty appears to be determined by two conditions: (a) general definitions of honesty and (b) consistent reinforcement for honest behavior. To develop a general trait of honesty, people must acquire broad general definitions of what honest and dishonest behavior are, and know which principles should be used to classify future situations. Furthermore, they need to be consistently reinforced for honest behavior until their standards of honesty have been internalized and they are intrinsically rewarded for honest conduct.

This research suggests that honesty is a personality trait that helps to identify individual differences. Individuals with a generalized trait of high personal integrity should behave honestly in almost all situations, regardless of the pressures and opportunities to benefit from dishonesty. Individuals with low personal integrity, on the other hand, might behave honestly or dishonestly depending on the situation. Normally they would be expected to act dishonestly, but if the chances of being caught are high and the punishment severe, they will probably act honestly. If the opportunities to defraud are inconvenient, or if the individuals have learned to be honest in particular situations, they again will probably behave honestly. However, in any given situation, they are more likely to behave dishonestly than individuals with high personal integrity. Consequently, individuals with high personal integrity should be the ones selected to fill important positions of trust. The likelihood of dishonesty is considerably less for individuals who have acquired a generalized trait of high personal integrity.

MEASURING HONESTY

Being able to measure personal integrity is important for selecting individuals to fill positions of trust. It is also important when inventory shrinkage of other records indicate that serious losses are occurring. While the evidence required to point an accusing finger must be greater than for selecting a person to trust, both situations illustrate the need for measuring personal integrity.

Several approaches have been developed for determining if an employee can be trusted with company funds. Polygraph or "lie detector" tests, vocal stress analysis, investigations of a person's background, and other psychological tests have been developed for measuring personal integrity.

Polygraph or "Lie Detector"

The polygraph measures an individual's autonomic responses while answering a fixed set of questions. These physiological responses include such things as pulse rate, blood pressure, galvanic skin resistance, rate and depth of respiration, and restlessness. The theory behind the use of the polygraph is simple: the emotional stress created by lying is reflected by significant autonomic changes, such as accelerated pulse, elevated blood pressure, and shallow and arrested respiration.

The validity of polygraph tests has been generally high. It has been determined that polygraph examiners will determine guilt accurately (when compared to later confessions or court findings) in 75 to 95 percent of their judgements (Horvath and Reid, 1971; Hunter and Ash, 1973).

Reid and Inbau (1966) stated that the polygraph has demonstrated its great utility in the investigation of thefts by employees in private industry and public employment and in the screening of applicants for employment in sensitive positions of trust. However, Rice (1978) has determined that even when all employees are tested annually, "all" generally means lower-level employees and not executives, even though it is the executives who are in the positions of greatest trust. Ferguson (1971) reported the findings of the polygraph pre-employment screening of three companies during a one-year period. These findings clearly demonstrated the importance of a thorough pre-employment interview. The following problems were found in applicants:

Categories	Number	Percent
Arrests	82	16
Unstable work record	30	6
Wants only short-term job	10	2
Fired from previous jobs	15	3
Major employee thefts	64	13
Personal/domestic problems	11	2
Health defects	15	3
Mental problems	31	6
Use of "hard" narcotics	16	3
Other problems	30	6

Business Week (1978) reports that fully one-fifth of the nation's largest companies use lie detectors. However, there are some groups, such as unions, that oppose their use. Yet, according to the same *Business Week* article, union locals quite actively use polygraphs in conducting their own investigations. An unfortunate constraint is that some states have passed laws forbidding companies from using polygraph tests for personnel decisions.

One difficulty in using the lie detector for pre-employment screening is that the percentage of persons being polygraphed who are telling lies is considerably lower than in criminal uses. Therefore, in pre-employment use, the number of false-positives (applicants rejected who shouldn't be) will be higher (Lykken, 1974). Nevertheless, in the hands of a trained examiner, the polygraph test is a highly-respected method of determining facts in a certain situation. Ferguson (1971) lists the following reasons why firms should use the polygraph, since it:

1. Results in better and/or more honest employees
2. Acts as a constant deterrent to employee dishonesty
3. Protects innocent employees from false accusations or suspicion
4. Determines who is guilty when thefts arise
5. Eliminates the narcotic addict, job jumper, chronic alcoholic, accident prone individuals, and habitual thieves
6. Eliminates poor security risks
7. Permits basically honest employees to work in harmony with their counterparts

He did, however, omit the most compelling reason: that it is much cheaper to use the polygraph than to financially support the criminal activities of employees.

Voice Stress Analysis

Another method for measuring employees' or prospective employees' evasiveness, lying, and guilt is voice stress analysis (*Business Week*, 1978). Just as the polygraph records stress through the autonomic responses of heart rate, respiration, blood pressure, and galvanic skin response, the voice-stress analyzer detects variations of a microtremor in the voice, which are autonomic nervous system reactions to stress. Three such instruments presently on the market are the Mark II, the PSE, and the Hagoth. In some unbiased tests of their validity, these machines have not lived up to expectations. For instance, an article in *Psychology Today* reports:

> In reputable studies of actual criminal suspects, whose guilt or innocence was later determined by confession or trial, voice analyzers have proven accurate in only 50 to 60 percent of the cases, a bit better than chance (Rice, 1978).

It appears that the voice stress analyzer is not as accurate as the polygraph. Nevertheless, many business executives have used it effectively in spite of its limitations. A restaurant chain uses voice stress analysis of taped annual interviews with employees. Even though employees know that the analysis is not completely accurate, the fact that they will be interviewed each year and possibly identified has significantly reduced food losses.

Other devices to determine the body's reaction to stress when lying, such as measuring pupil size, blood volume, skin temperature, facial expressions, body language, brain waves, etc., are presently being investigated. Perhaps the most promising and productive area of research, however, is in replacing the polygraph operator with a computer that analyzes the results.

Background Investigations

A widely-used method of investigation, especially of potential applicants to new jobs involving positions of trust, is a background check. This is usually accomplished by gathering information from police records, retail credit bureaus, employment histories, and interviews with past associates. The person's desirability as a hiring risk is inferred indirectly from this composite information.

Even though background investigations are used extensively, the investigations conducted are often incomplete. This incompleteness or lack of thoroughness of the investigation is the major defect in background investigations. Background investigations do not pinpoint the individuals who have not yet become one of the "one-time" offenders, since they do not yet have a criminal record. However, they can uncover such things as poor credit ratings, financial stress, questionable background, mental problems, and "wheeler-dealer" tendencies. In short, the background investigations can uncover many of the personal characteristics red flags (Romney and Albrecht, 1979).

Psychological Instruments

Several psychological instruments have been developed to measure personal integrity. These paper and pencil questionnaires are primarily used to evaluate the hiring risk of new employees; however, they have also been used as a check on the honesty of present employees. These instruments are marketed through various consulting organizations that provide the questionnaires, analyze the results, and prepare recommendations.

One questionnaire that has been used extensively in measuring employees who are potential embezzlers is the Reid Report (Reid, 1967; Ash, 1971). The Reid Report (John E. Reid & Associates, 215 N. Dearborn Street, Chicago, IL 60601) has been developed for employers to use as a selection tool in hiring new employees who will fill positions of trust. Considerable research on over 5,000 job applicants has shown that the Reid Report is highly reliable (.90 and above; Ash, 1970, 1971, 1976) and produces scores that are correlated about .60 with polygraph test scores. Not only does it appear to be a good measure of personal honesty, it does not have an adverse impact on minorities, females, or older applicants. In fact, the honesty scores of older individuals and females were usually slightly higher. Furthermore, the evidence seems to indicate that individuals tend to provide honest answers even when it involves admission of previous dishonesty. (Perhaps their honesty was due in part to the knowledge of a subsequent polygraph test).

Another instrument for measuring honesty is the Personnel Selection Inventory (PSI). The PSI (London House Management Consultants, 1550 Northwest Highway, Park Ridge, IL 60068) has also been shown to have no adverse impact on the hiring of applicants from any racial or ethnic group. Studies have shown that the dishonesty scale of the PSI is correlated with the admitted amount of on-the-job theft. Two other instruments similar to the Reid Report and the PSI are the Stanton Survey (The Stanton Corporation, 407 South Dearborn St., Chicago, IL 60605) and the T.A. Survey (Trustworthiness Attitude; Personnel Security Corporation, 1301 West 22nd Street, Suite 702, Oak Brook, IL 60521). All four of these instruments are widely used and the producers of each instrument can provide evidence showing their usefulness.

The four instruments above all focus specifically on measuring honesty. Other instruments measuring various personality characteristics have also been used to assess the likelihood of fraud and dishonesty. As noted earlier, the California Psychological Inventory, the Minnesota Multiphasic Personality Inventory, and the Bipolar Psychological Inventory have been used to measure dishonesty and criminal traits. The California Psychological Inventory is a very popular personality test that has been widely used for many purposes (Consulting Psychologists, 577 College Avenue, Palo Alto, CA 94306). Our study found significant differences between college students and fraud perpetrators on certain scales of the Bipolar Psychological Inventory (BPI; Diagnostic Specialist Inc., 1170 North 660 West, Orem, UT 84057). This would indicate that the BPI might be used as a personnel screening device. Those with a raw score above five on the Lie scale, above six on the Psychic Pain scale, and above five on the Social Deviancy scale have a higher probability of having similar characteristics to our fraud perpetrator group. These three scales might represent what is discussed elsewhere in this book: the Lie scale identifies the dishonest person, the Psychic Pain scale measures the non-sharable problem, and the Social Deviancy scale measures criminal behavior, thinking, and rationalization. The L (lie); K (defensiveness); and Pd (psychoanalyticdeviate) scales of the MMPI might similarly be used (MMPI Psychological Corporation, 757 Third Avenue, New York, NY 10017).

* SUMMARY POINTS OF CHAPTER 9 *

* Most fraud perpetrators are not incarcerated; hence, it is difficult to empirically study their personal characteristics.
* Fraud perpetrators are an extremely heterogenous group and do not have a common personality profile.
* A pilot study conducted by the authors shows that fraud perpetrators are distinguished from other property offenders on several demographic factors and personality characteristics.
* Three methods to assess employee trust are:
    1) polygraph or "lie detector" tests
    2) background investigations
    3) psychological tests measuring personal integrity.

10

PERSONNEL POLICIES AND PRACTICES THAT REDUCE FRAUD: A SUMMARY

Chapter 10 Explains:

- Strategies for reducing situational pressures.
- Strategies for reducing fraud opportunities.
- Strategies for increasing personal integrity.
- Social forces contributing to fraud.

The three factors that produce fraud were described in Chapter 2. These three forces include situational pressure, opportunities to commit fraud, and personal integrity. The decision to commit fraud results from an interaction of these three factors. Situational pressures refer to the immediate pressures individuals experience within their environments. Opportunities to commit fraud refer to opportunities that individuals create for themselves, as well as opportunities created by the company through careless internal controls. Personal integrity refers to the personal code of ethical behavior that each person adopts.

The three factors that produce fraud were illustrated in Exhibit 2-1 (p. 39). This model shows how the decision to commit fraud is determined by the interaction of all three forces. A useful way to visualize the interaction is to picture a balance scale with three connecting bars. Each of the three connected bars has a weight that can move in either direction independently of the other weights. Thus, the sizes of each weight and their locations along the three bars determine which side of the scale is heaviest.

This is an additive model where the scales become tipped

in favor of committing fraud when any combination of the three weights has moved far enough. Some have suggested that the model should be reconstructed as an interactive model, where certain minimum levels on each factor have to be exceeded before the other factors can tip the scales toward a fraudulent act. Specifically, some have claimed that personal integrity must be compromised to some degree before opportunities and pressures can entice an individual to be dishonest. Perhaps it should be treated as an interactive model, but our interviews with white-collar criminals seemed to imply an additive model. Some white-collar criminals appeared to have exceptionally high personal integrity. "If you only knew the situation I was in," some stated, "you would have understood why I did it. Any man would have done the same."

REDUCING FRAUD

The three factors illustrated in Exhibit 2-1 provide a useful framework for diagnosing fraud and taking corrective action to reduce it. In short, fraud is reduced by limiting the pressures and opportunities to commit fraud and increasing personal integrity. If organizational leaders are sufficiently concerned about the possibilities of fraud in their companies, there are several actions they can take. The following ideas are possible actions for managers to consider. Some factors, such as executive financial disclosure, may not be very popular. Managers should only adopt changes that seem necessary for their situations. As the potential losses from fraud or the opportunities to commit fraud increase, more factors ought to be considered.

Reduce Situational Pressures. In the free enterprise system, it is neither possible nor even desirable to eliminate all situational pressures. A moderate level of pressure on individuals, departments, and companies is desirable. At times, however, the pressures become overwhelming. Escape outlets, like pressure valves, must be provided.

1. Avoid setting unrealistically high performance expectations. Companies that set arbitrary goals for increased earnings, sales, or profits with a "do it at any cost" attitude encourage managers to behave dishonestly, especially during

times of economic downturns. An excellent method for avoiding unrealistic performance goals is to involve employees in setting their own goals. Several studies have found that participation in goal setting and budgeting has significantly increased the level of motivation and commitment for success, since the employees feel like they "own" the responsibility.

2. Remove unnecessary obstacles blocking effective performance, such as obsolete equipment or inventory, insufficient working capital, and excess capacity. Severe obsolescence of equipment and personal skills can be avoided with adequate planning. Insufficient working capital and excess production capacity are also problems created by inadequate planning. Good forecasting and advance preparation can also minimize some of the pressures created by cost increases, difficulty in collecting receivables, unusually heavy competition, or tax adjustments by the IRS.

3. Provide personal counseling to help employees with financial problems. Employee assistance programs in many companies have been very effective in helping employees with personal problems. Alcoholism, drug abuse, marital problems, and gambling often create financial problems and reduced work effectiveness. These intense pressures, which often lead employees to commit fraud, ¢an be reduced by an effective assistance program that helps employees manage their finances and redirect their lives. Large companies can develop their own employee assistance programs. Small companies may want to contract with private companies to provide employee assistance services. Literature on these programs is available through most local personnel associations or in personnel administration literature such as The Personnel Administrator.

4. Establish fair and uniform personnel policies. Fraud has occasionally been committed by employees because of a feeling of revenge or resentment of their superiors. Because they feel underpaid, are passed over for promotion, or are treated unfairly, some employees defraud their company with a belief that they are only getting even. In one case, a manager chose to ignore a $2,500 per year theft from the petty cash account because he knew the employee was underpaid by at least $5,000 per year (Zeitlin, 1971).

Jaspan (1972) indicated that many managers show favoritism or violate their own sets of procedures and policies. He suggested that such violation is extremely detrimental to attitudes within a firm and claimed that nothing else can break down discipline and morale, or lessen respect for management so rapidly. Leibholz and Wilson (1974) suggested that there should especially be specific policies in the area of terminations. They suggest that terminations should be handled politely and quickly, thus preventing the employees from having the time to seek revenge on the corporation. Carson (1977) also added that to encourage honesty, all personnel policies and practices should be uniform and apply equally to all employees. He suggested that there should be no favoritism shown to friends or relatives. Finally, the U.S. Chamber of Commerce (1974) indicated that unfair and inconsistant personnel policies lead to frustration, and frustration leads to employee dishonesty. The need for fair and uniform personnel policies that are equitably administered is very apparent for more reasons than just to reduce fraud.

Reduce Opportunities. An elaborate security system and tight internal controls are usually considered a necessity for reducing fraud. While such programs are not the total solution to the problem, fraud can be reduced by making it more difficult to do or to hide. The following factors should reduce the opportunities to commit fraud.

1. Carefully monitor the business transactions and interpersonal relationships of suppliers, buyers, purchasing agents, sales representatives and others who interface in the transactions between financial units. These individuals are constantly faced with situations in which subjective business decisions can easily result in illegal bribes, kickbacks, and payoffs, or in favors and gifts that might be unethical, even if they are legal.

2. Maintain accurate and complete internal accounting records. The accounting department needs to be adequately staffed with competent professionals. The internal accounting system must be carefully designed to monitor all business transactions and it must operate efficiently with timely and accurate reports.

3. Establish a physical security system to secure the assets of the company, including finished goods, cash, equipment,

tools, and other items of worth. A good security system requires a detailed analysis of each company's physical assets and
the flow of its materials. Fraud is especially troublesome during transportation and at loading docks.

4. Do not rely solely on one individual to perform an important function. The opportunity to commit fraud is especially prevalent when one employee has total control over an
operation that no one else observes or understands. Many
computer-related frauds have been discovered only by accident. Executives and other key employees are sometimes capable of controlling a single function that enables them to
embezzle funds. To reduce this problem, executives should be
required to take an annual vacation, during which time other
individuals perform their functions. Job rotation and temporary assignments are also useful in teaching other employees
how to perform important functions, as well as acting as a
check against improper actions.

5. Maintain accurate personnel records regarding the previous backgrounds and current financial activities of employees. This information might include the employees' criminal
records, police records, improper actions on their present jobs,
statements from previous employers, evidence of living beyond their present income levels, expensive habits or tastes,
and even a complete financial disclosure of the employees'
personal wealth. Requiring each employee to make a full financial disclosure each year is not a very popular practice and
some employees may consider it an invasion of privacy. However, executives and individuals who hold positions of trust
would probably understand the need for financial disclosures
which would make instances of material fraud apparent.

6. Develop strong leadership and cohesive work groups.
Each employee should feel a personal identification with a
work group directed by a capable leader. Through effective
supervision, internal controls and company procedures can be
enforced tactfully and fairly. Identification with a cohesive
work group reduces the tendency to think that fraud is not
hurting anyone because the company is a large, impersonal
corporation. Strong leadership also creates greater awareness
of personal problems and other pressures that create fraud.

Strengthen Personal Integrity. Fraud is a dishonest act

committed by individuals. Regardless of the situational pressures and opportunities to commit fraud, the dishonest act is still committed by the individual and society holds individuals accountable for their behavior. As individuals adopt a strong code of personal ethics and internalize a standard of high personal integrity, the probability that they will commit a fraud is reduced.

1. Managers should teach honesty by induction and modeling. Honesty is a moral behavior and research on moral development suggests that induction and modeling are effective techniques for acquiring moral behaviors. Induction refers to teaching and explaining, which could encompass any form of instruction such as lectures, group discussions, written material, "thoughts for the day," or casual comments. Modeling refers to the example that is set by important individuals, such as organizational leaders or close co-workers. If top management is dishonest in their associations with the public or government agencies, other staff members are more inclined to also be dishonest. To create an environment of honesty, managers must eliminate every form of dishonesty in all areas of their business practices such as: sales, advertising, expense accounts, price setting, purchasing, returned merchandise or broken equipment, and every other facet of business activity.

2. Honest and dishonest behavior needs to be defined. For example, most purchasing agents would agree that accepting a $5,000 bribe from a supplier is dishonest, but what about a weekend vacation at a hunting cabin? A major cause of dishonesty comes from rationalizing and redefining the situation. It is natural for the criteria of expediency to replace the criteria of right versus wrong. To avoid this problem, it is necessary to set explicit standards of conduct and general principles of behavior defining what is honest and dishonest. Many corporations have recently adopted an explicit code of conduct that all managers are required to read, sign, and follow.

3. Select honest employees to occupy positions of trust. Several instruments have been designed to measure the personal integrity of job applicants, such as the Reid Report and the Personnel Security Inventory. The evidence showing that these scales can reliably predict personal integrity is rather impressive. In the employment interview, the candidates could

be asked directly if they are honest and trustworthy. Such a question signals to the candidate the importance of honesty to the company.

4. Develop an organizational climate that emphasizes the importance of honesty. Such a climate can be established through subtle methods, such as identifying top management's errors and mistakes, and acknowledging them in company newsletters. It can also be established through explicit methods, such as a formal presentation included in a new employee orientation program. Top management ought to make it clear that honest reports are more important than favorable reports.

5. The consequences of violating the rules and the punishment of fraud perpetrators should not be kept secret. Even though white-collar crime is an embarrassment to a company, failing to uncover fraud and prosecute offenders contributes to its increase. Employees who have been quietly dismissed for fraud in one company often go to another company and continue their dishonest ways. The general perception of many individuals is that many white-collar crimes are never discovered, especially computer fraud; when they are discovered, the offenders are not prosecuted, and if they are prosecuted, the penalties are not very heavy. In general, these perceptions are correct. While severe penalties do not totally eliminate crime, the severity of the penalty does act as a deterrent of crime.

A Unified Assault on Fraud

Most previous suggestions for reducing fraud have focused on eliminating the opportunities to commit fraud through tighter security. Long lists of suggestions have been compiled describing elaborate physical security systems and internal accounting control systems. Such programs should definitely reduce fraud, but they are not the total solution to the fraud problem. The model described earlier suggests that fraud may still occur even though external security and internal controls appear to eliminate opportunities. If individuals are dishonest, or if they have a sufficient need, they will create their own opportunities. A reduction in fraud requires a combined thrust of simultaneously reducing the opportunity and situational pressures to defraud, along with increasing personal integrity.

A successful assault on the fraud problem cannot be a half-hearted or hypocritical effort. The suggestions listed above clearly illustrate how management has the capacity either to reduce fraud or to increase it by the policies and procedures they adopt. Regardless of whether their influence is intended or not, the behavior of managers can increase or decrease the likelihood of material fraud. While managers may be reluctant to play the role of social moralists, it is obvious that their actions exert a powerful influence over the behavior of organization members. Since honesty is such a widely-accepted social value and the costs of fraud are so enormous, we think it is imperative that managers assume a greater responsibility for positive actions that reduce fraud. Corporate leaders ought to join the accounting profession and other social organizations in launching an assault on fraud. Effective changes in auditing and business practices, when reinforced with supportive organizational and social changes, can significantly reduce fraud.

SOCIAL FORCES CONTRIBUTING TO FRAUD

Many of the forces contributing to fraud are outside the walls of the organization. These forces are not controlled by a single organization; they are social forces that are influenced by political and economic conditions and social expectations. The remainder of this chapter discusses several societal factors that have tended to contribute, either directly or indirectly, to an increase in fraud by reducing its costs and increasing its benefits. As illustrated in Exhibit 10-1, eight societal factors have been classified into two groups: (1) social conditions and (2) actions that society fails to take. If fraud is to be controlled, society as a whole must take corrective action against these eight factors.

Exhibit 10-1

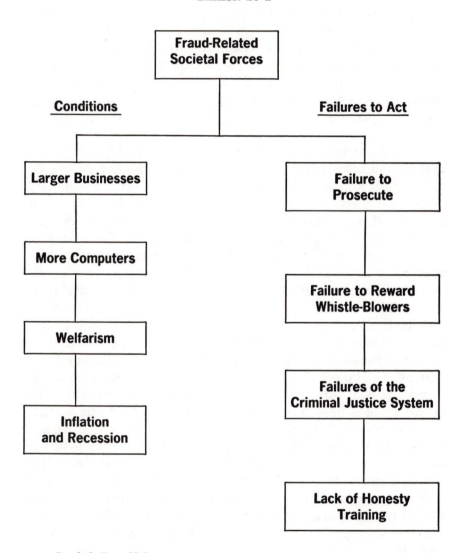

Social Conditions

The Increased Size of Firms. There are at least three ways in which larger size contributes to an increase in fraud. First, being a member of a larger unit creates an anonymity that reduces the chances of being caught or punished. People are more likely to commit fraud when they believe that it will be difficult to trace the fraud to them.

A second way in which increased organizational size contributes to fraud is that it makes people either apathetic or antagonistic toward the organization. These attitudes often lead to what is called the "Robin Hood Syndrome." This is a condition in which perpetrators feel that doing harm to people is highly immoral, but doing harm to large institutions is not wrong because they are so large that they won't miss what is taken from them (Morgensen, 1976; Nycum, 1975). In other words, robbing from the rich to give to the poor is not wrong, and it's especially nice if the perpetrator is the one who is poor.

A third reason why increased organizational size contributes to fraud is explained by the concept of the "agency theory" (Jensen and Meckling, 1975). Most firms are managed by individuals who own only a small fraction of the firm's outstanding shares. This situation implies a conflict of interest among firm managers and external investors. For example, consider the case of a firm in which the manager owns only a fraction of its outstanding shares. If the manager were to divert the firm's resources to his own use, allow lax discipline among his subordinates, or embezzle, the marginal cost of such activities to the manager would be only a fraction of the total resources involved. The manager, however, would reap the total benefits of these alternative-resource misappropriations. If a manager is a "self-utility maximizer," (i.e., he maximizes his own advantage) he will allocate firm resources to satisfy his own desires until the marginal expected utility from doing so just equals the marginal cost. The remaining, larger fraction of the cost will be imposed upon the firm's external owners. This same argument can be used to suggest that often a manager has incentives to falsify reports, since he realizes that his performance will be evaluated with this information. By falsifying reports, he can continue to maximize his utility, and the shareholders may not be able to discover that he is diverting resources to himself.

Computers and Fraud. Several people (e.g., Gilson, 1975) have argued that the increased use of computers has enhanced the opportunity to perpetrate and conceal frauds. Gilson suggested that traditional measures for internal control are ineffective or difficult to accomplish in a computer age. This is especially true because the development of both the laws regulating computers and the safeguards for computers have often lagged behind other developments in computer technology. Finally, it has previously been suggested that many people view the computer as an impersonal object that can justifiably be abused. Donn Parker (1975) of Stanford Research Institute published a computer abuse study based on 375 reported cases. In this report, he dealt with several aspects of computer abuse, one of which was a profile of the perpetrators. His profile was based on interviews with 17 of the offenders involved in 15 reported abuse cases. Although this population was not selected on a random basis, and therefore might not be representative of all cases, the characteristics of the perpetrators were interesting. Twelve of these perpetrators felt that it was immoral to harm people, but did not feel that any harm was done by computer fraud. Gottheimer (1978) also indicated that, to many people, the computer symbolizes a system of uncaring power that tends not only to instill efforts to strike back at the machine, but also to offer a set of convenient rationalizations for engaging in fraudulent activities. After all, he continued, stealing from a large corporation by means of a machine is impersonal and carries none of the potential violence of the personal confrontation that comes with conventional thievery. Waller (1975) indicated that people believe it somehow is not the company's money, but rather just "Monopoly-money" in the computer, when the computer is the instrument used in perpetrating the fraud.

The Welfare State and Fraud. Comer (1977) stated that there is an increased permissiveness in society that has allowed more and more people to be able to justify illegal activities and see crime as the answer to their problems. Crime, like welfare, is another way of getting something for nothing. He suggested that many free countries are becoming more like welfare states and that this increased welfarism or acceptance of egalitarian ideas makes it easier for people to rationalize the misappropriation of corporate assets as a way of sharing the wealth.

Inflation and Recession. Inflation and recession create pressures that cause otherwise honest people to commit fraudulent activities. Many people who are in responsible positions find their salaries and personal incomes eroded by inflation, and thus see their positions of trust as opportunities to commit fraud and resolve their financial problems. Many people feel helpless when confronting the problems of increasing prices, high interest rates, the slow-down of the economy, and increased joblessness. They see striking back by committing fraud as an acceptable means of easing the pressures by getting even with government, business, or whomever else they see as responsible for their problems.

Social Actions

Failure of Businesses to Prosecute. The literature contains numerous references indicating that businesses either fail or decide not to prosecute fraud perpetrators (U.S. Chamber of Commerce, 1974; Nolan, 1974; Gottheimer, 1978; Stone and Mason, 1978; Meyers, 1975; Freed, 1969; Russell, 1975; and Klein and Densmore, 1977). Most of these authors suggest that businesses treat employee and executive fraud as an expected cost of doing business. In fact, Klein and Densmore (1977) stated that only 12 percent of all detected fraud leads to the prosecution or dismissal of the perpetrators. They further indicated that only 5 percent of all detected frauds result in conviction, and only one percent of the perpetrators are actually incarcerated. When these estimates are coupled with those of undetected fraud (85 percent of computer-based crimes have yet to be discovered), the odds certainly seem to favor the perpetrators.

Firms give several reasons for choosing not to prosecute. For example, they say they fear the adverse publicity that would result if the public discovered there was fraud in the firms. They are afraid that if the public were made aware of a fraud, they would suspect that the firms were negligent in not detecting the fraud sooner, and the result would be adverse publicity, possible litigation, increased regulatory restrictions, or adverse consumer reaction. Another reason proposed by firms for their failure to prosecute is the fear of counter-suits for such things as libel, malicious prosecution, false arrest, etc., by the perpetrators. Even with these fears, however, probably the single-most significant reason for nonprosecution is that it is not economically feasible to prosecute employees and executives caught in criminal activities. It usually takes a significant amount of time and money to prosecute, and the rewards gained by prosecution are minimal.

Psychologically, the effect of failing to prosecute is to reward dishonest behavior. Middlebrook (1974) suggests that the effect of no punishment is a signal to everyone that the cost of dishonesty is not very high.

Ostracism of the Whistle-Blower. Another factor that seems to contribute to increased fraud is ostracism of the whistle-blower (informant). There have been several instances in which the only individuals who suffered from a fraud case were the whistle-blowers.

An example of this phenomenon was seen in a CPA firm whose accountants informed one of their clients that his employees were committing fraud. Their reward for this disclosure was dismissal as the firm's auditors (Brief, 1977). Several interesting examples of ostracizing informants in government were included in an article called "Buying and Selling at the Pentagon" (Miller, 1978). One of the cases noted was that of a meat-grader, Dick C., who found evidence of widespread fraud when the Department of Agriculture sent him to Chicago. Working with the F.B.I., Dick C. forced the resignation of more than 70 percent of the city's meat-graders on corruption charges. The reward for his actions was that he set a record for the longest tenure in the service without a promotion: 26 years. Another example was that of an engineer, David S., who made price evaluations on the purchases of small items from the defense construction supply center at Columbus, Ohio. He believed that local suppliers and his supervisors were using charges far in excess of reasonable market cost. When he complained to his supervisors, David S. was temporarily suspended and received his first unsatisfactory performance rating in 15 years of government service. Finally, after taking his case to the news media, he was removed from his job for insubordination.

While, at first, these incidents of whistle-blowing were thought to be isolated and not indicative of the general condition, it was often the whistle-blower who suffered from the occurrence of fraud. The effects of ostracism result in fewer frauds being disclosed.

The Criminal-Justice System and Fraud. There are several inefficiencies in the criminal-justice system that contribute to an increase in fraud. With respect to prosecution and its associated costs, Blustein (1978) stated that the criminal system all too often lets fraud perpetrators go free, for one or more of the following reasons: highly-placed connections, bribes, judges who are reluctant to condemn middle-class people to prison terms, or high-priced lawyers who know all the tricks. He argued that such lawyers, using a variety of delay tactics, can make the prosecution of fraud extremely expensive and time-consuming. Because of these high costs, many U.S. attorneys won't even prosecute a case involving a few thousand dollars. Instead, they recommend that embezzlers be quietly fired, since that is the only economically feasible alternative.

A second justice-related factor contributing to increased fraud is the inadequate punishment given to fraud perpetrators. Judge John Lord, when sentencing convicted school suppliers in the early 1960s, stated: "All are God-fearing men, highly civic-minded, who have spent lifetimes in sincere and honest dedication and service to their families, their churches, their country, and their communities. I could never send Mr. _____ to jail" (Morgensen, 1975). In a 1974 symposium on crime and business, Jack Anderson was quoted as saying that the average sentence for a perpetrator of fraud was one year in jail for every $10 million stolen. Concerning this problem, an agent in the F.B.I.'s fraud department said that there are problems of attitude when law enforcement is confronted with computer or other fraud perpetrators. The law enforcement community views fraud quite differently from the way it does violent crime; they tend to see it as a civil matter instead. As a result, judges find it hard to perceive as a criminal a defendent who might have a background similar to his or her own.

There are several examples of fraud perpetrators getting extremely light sentences. The president of an oil company spent a grand total of one night in jail for his fraud. Robert S., who defrauded Pacific Telephone and Telegraph of $1 million in electronics equipment, spent 40 days in jail and settled out of court for $8,500. Probably the most notable instance, however, is the president of a San Diego bank, who, after being accused of misplacing over $200 million, received a sentence of four years probation and a $30,000 fine payable at $100 a month for 25 years, without interest.

Another example is the Computer Corp. case (Littrell, 1980). During the period when its name played on Wall Street's fascination with both leisure and computer stocks, the corporation claimed assets of $51 million in its audited financial statements. Only two years later, however, in the criminal trial of the corporation's officers, evidence indicated that it had almost no bona fide assets. The company's biggest asset, booked at $32 million, was a claim to 20 percent of the oil under 3.5 million acres of the Arctic Ocean. The corporation told its shareholders that it put out marker-buoys and had dog sleds diligently patrolling its claims. A long-closed greyhound track in Arizona, with no license and little prospect of getting one, was booked at $2.2 million for stock. For its stockholders' benefit, the corporation announced a 60-day racing season. Then there were the 5,000 acres in California's Imperial Valley carried as a $1.3 million asset. That prime agricultural land happened, however, to also be occupied by an Army gunnery range. The corporation may have distributed publicly, or used for collateral, some 25 million shares at prices ranging to $11 per share. Following the trial, the defendants were found guilty of 12 counts of securities and mail fraud and conspiracy. Three months later, they were sentenced to terms ranging from only three months to one year in prison, but were not fined.

Lack of Honesty Training. Investigators blame the increases in fraud on a number of factors. Among those reasons is the erosion of moral standards. Many people argue that this erosion of standards is attributed to the lack of honesty training in our society. As evidence of this, Comer (1977) cited the fact that more than one-half of the people arrested for indictable offenses in London were under 21. Almost one-third of the number were between 10 and 16. In addition, criminal behavior in schools is running at an alarming rate. Many of the executives we visited suggested that neither schools, churches, nor families teach integrity as rigorously today as they did in past generations. If this is true, we may have a serious problem, because, as argued by Burton (1963), there exists a general trait of honesty only in those individuals whose parents (and others) have consistently reinforced them for honest acts.

* SUMMARY POINTS OF CHAPTER 10 *

* Fraud is influenced by an interaction of three forces:
  1) situational pressures
  2) opportunities
  3) personal characteristics.
* Societal forces resulting in increased fraud include:
  1) failure to prosecute
  2) larger business
  3) ostracizism of the whistle-blower
  4) more computers

     5) failure of the criminal justice system
     6) lack of honesty training
     7) welfarism
     8) inflation.

* Society and organizations within society can reduce fraud by:
     1) prosecuting fraud perpetrators
     2) rewarding firms that prosecute fraud perpetrators
     3) minimizing the adverse publicity received by firms who prosecute perpetrators
     4) providing legal assistance and support to smaller firms concerned about counter-suits
     5) publicizing the discipline given fraud perpetrators
     6) decreasing the anonymity of employees
     7) making employees feel like they are an important part of an organization
     8) educating employees and management about the need to report dishonest behavior
     9) rewarding informers
     10) maintaining adequate administrative, operational, processing, and documentation controls over computer operations
     11) segregating the duties of computer personnel
     12) publishing computer abuse guidelines
     13) identifying the legal limits of computer use
     14) passing specific laws to punish computer criminals
     15) giving convicted fraud perpetrators stiffer penalties commensurate with the dollar loss involved in the crime
     16) speeding up the judicial process to make fraud prosecution more cost-beneficial
     17) providing honesty and ethics training for managers
     18) making honesty important in the company
     19) encouraging the teaching of honesty and integrity at home, in school, and in church
     20) having each employee sign an annual statement that he or she hasn't committed fraud or doesn't know of anyone who has
     21) setting an honest example
     22) reestablishing, as much as possible, the work ethic and eliminating the "get something for nothing" attitude that often exists
     23) paying employees an adequate wage
     24) assisting employees in coping with the pressures of inflation and/or recession.

APPENDIX A
THEORETICAL
EXPLANATIONS
OF CRIME AND
FRAUD

This Appendix Explains:

- Physiological theories of crime.
- Psychological theories of crime.
- Internal and external variables related to fraud.
- Sociological theories of crime.
- Learning fraudulent behavior.
- Personal characteristics.
- Need for multiple theories of fraud.

This appendix reviews the various concepts and theories used to explain crime in general and fraud in particular. Several disciplines, such as psychology, sociology, criminology, and business, have described fraud from their own perspectives, emphasizing different aspects of the problem. Based on the authors' data and a review of these perspectives, it is our position that fraud results from the interaction of forces within the individual's personality and the influences of the external environment. This position is consistent with our list of red flags, which includes (a) situational factors, (b) opportunities to commit fraud, and (c) personality characteristics. These three dimensions include most of the findings and observations related to fraud.

A study of fraud and the fraud perpetrator must address the following questions: Which personality traits or internal factors contribute to fraudulent acts? To what extent are external variables and social forces significant in the commission of

199

fraud? Does any one explanation seem superior to others in accounting for fraud? Can current theories of criminality and deviant behavior be used to understand fraud? In this appendix, we review the general theories of criminality that have attempted to provide answers to these questions. This review, by necessity, is quite broad and includes a discussion of the general theories of crime.

GENERAL THEORIES OF CRIMINALITY

The search for a single theory of criminality or fraudulent behavior often assumes the existence of a homogeneous group. The only characteristic all criminals seem to have in common is that they have committed and/or have been found guilty of committing a crime. Beyond that, there do not appear to be any general characteristics that *all* criminals share. Persons who commit fraud, for example, are quite different from those who commit aggravated assault or forcible rape. Another reality is the fact that specific situations and social pressures may be as relevant as the offender's character.

Over the past three centuries, several attempts have been made to determine the general causes of criminality. Gibbons' (1973) *Society, Crime, and Criminal Careers*, analyzed these general theories of criminality and classified them into (a) physiological, (b) psychological, and (c) sociological explanations of crime. He concluded that no single theory can explain all the complex forms of crime. Instead, he has suggested that different forms of crime, which he called criminal careers, should be examined separately.

Physiological Explanations of Crime

One of the best-known early physiological explanations for crime came from Lombroso (1835-1909), an Italian physician. Lombroso was asked to perform an autopsy on a noted criminal. In the course of the autopsy, he discovered a number of physical abnormalities in the criminal's brain. Being impressed with these observations, Lombroso formulated the view that criminals were atavists, or genetic throwbacks to a primitive form of human species. He maintained that the degenerate criminal type could be identified by a number of characteristics, including facial asymmetry, eye defects, ear peculiarities, excessively long arms, and other physical abnormalities.

Lombroso's ideas were published in *The Criminal Man*, which went through five separate editions (Vold, 1958). In later editions, numerous other criminal causal factors were mentioned and added to the notion of reversion to a primitive biological type. In the early 1900s, Lombroso's physiological explanation was thoroughly discredited by Goring's (1913) study of 3,000 English convicts. Careful measurements of these convicts and a large number of non-convicts revealed, almost without exception, that Lombroso's hypothetical physical anomalies were no more common among convicts than among non-convicts. Several other biological explanations of crime have met the same discrediting fate, including Hooton's (1939) theory that crime is caused by biological inferiority in inherently inferior organisms, Sheldon's proposed linkages between delinquency and certain body types (Sheldon, Stevens, and Tucker, 1940), and other theories of hereditary transmission.

Future research might find specific biological factors that are consistently associated with crime. Present avenues of research are in the areas of endocrine, neurological, and chemical factors. For the present, however, one must conclude that crime does not appear to be caused by physiological factors.

Psychological Explanations of Crime

The most popular psychological explanations of crime are derived from psychodynamic theories. These explanations often assume that criminals behave as they do because they are in some way "sick" or "maladjusted." The environment may act as a precipitating factor, but it is seldom seen as the primary force in the causation of crime. At one time, mental disorders were viewed as the major causes of crime and a determined effort was made to diagnose the nature of the disorders. As greater sophistication was achieved in diagnosing abnormalities, the conclusion that criminality was caused by mental disorders was not found to be universally true.

Psychoanalytic theories—internal focus. Most explanations derived from Freud's psychoanalytic theory share a common assumption that behavior is largely the product of unconscious psychological-biological forces ("drives" or "instincts") that are not directly perceived by the person. One explanation claims that crime results from a conflict in the unconscious mind that produces feelings of guilt and anxiety, along with a consequent desire to remove the guilt feelings and restore a proper balance of good against evil. The person may commit a criminal act in order to be caught and punished. Unconsciously motivated errors (i.e., careless or imprudent ways of committing the crime) cause the person to leave "clues" to help authorities apprehend and convict the guilty, and thus administer suitable, cleansing punishment.

Psychoanalytic theory hypothesizes that there are three parts of the personality, the id, the ego, and the superego. The id, with its desire to satisfy wants immediately, is usually credited with criminal motivation. Criminal acts are committed by individuals who do not control the raw, uninhibited impulses of the id. Since most of the id's influence is from the subconscious or unconscious, the fraud perpetrator is seldom aware of the real influences or causes of his criminal activity. Freud believed that behavior is a consequence of developmental sequences that are regulated by innate characteristics and cumulative experiences. According to psychoanalytic thought, fraud could be caused by many factors, such as the failure of the individual to progress normally through the developmental stages. At a later time, and for various reasons, there may be a regression to an earlier developmental stage involving less control, tantrums, demands, and threats. Other possibilities leading to criminal behavior include unbridled biological drives, or detrimental past experiences, especially traumatic ones.

The superego, which is often equated with the "conscience," is the motivational drive that keeps the person from committing antisocial acts. It is generally believed that the conscience is learned from parents. This theory suggests that fraud results from an underdeveloped conscience, stemming from a lack of parental identification. Such crime might also be symptomatic of other underlying problems involving guilt, frustration, or conflict.

The ego is the part of the personality that interacts with external reality. The ego organizes the thought processes and governs actions. It mediates between the instinctual impulses of the id, the demands of the environment, and the standards of the superego. The theory is dynamic in nature, and recognizes the interaction between the personal needs of the individual and the external demands of reality. Conflicts between reality and personal needs are often acted out by the criminal.

There have been several psychoanalytic studies of general crime, but apparently none focused specifically on fraud. More importantly, however, psychoanalytic explanations for criminal behavior have been extensively criticized. Perhaps the greatest criticism concerns the inadequacy of the basic definitions of psychoanalytic concepts. A methodology such as psychoanalysis, under which only the patient knows the "facts" of the case and only the analyst understands the meaning of those "facts" as revealed to him by the patient, does not lend itself to external, third-person, impersonal verification, or to generalization beyond the limits of any particular case. In other words, psychoanalytic explanations are based upon the impressions and biases of the analyst. Thus, psychoanalytic theories are not generally very useful in studying fraud.

Learning theories—external focus. In contrast to psychoanalytic theory, learning theory claims that crime, like all behavior, is determined by the environmental setting according to principles of classical or operant conditioning. According to operant conditioning, individuals will do what they are reinforced for doing. If they are reinforced for being honest, they will be honest, and vice versa. Most fraudulent behavior is supposedly learned by operant conditioning. In other words, crime pays, and each time it pays, the related criminal behavior is reinforced. Criminal behaviors are also strengthened by the removal of noxious stimuli such as debts. The criminal's pro-social behaviors are weakened when he is punished following these pro-social behaviors (such as when his friends make fun of him for passing up an easy buck). His socially appropriate acts also become less prevalent when they precede the loss of some desired outcome; he stops gambling, but then his friends leave him, so he is inclined to continue gambling. Usually a person becomes a criminal by being reinforced for some small, illegal act that encourages him to do more. He is then shaped into more extensive criminality as he is rewarded for each subsequent act. The environment, including the people in it and its rewards and punishments, creates the resulting behavior.

The reinforcements or punishments do not have to be experienced directly; they can be experienced vicariously. The potential fraud perpetrator can see others getting rewards for their crimes, so he models their behavior. Or, he might imagine himself carrying out the criminal act and getting the reward; this fantasy reinforces him and increases the probability of his actually committing the crime. In most criminal activities, the criminal is reinforced by money or goods that can be exchanged for other reinforcements. He may also be reinforced by revenge, power, control, or even social approval.

The principles of operant conditioning have provided a useful theory for examining fraud. As will be shown later, Sutherland's theory of differential association is an application of operant conditioning principles to white-collar crime (Burgess and Akers, 1966). Behavior principles indicate that responses which are only intermittently reinforced, especially on a variable-ratio-reinforcement schedule, are more resistant to extinction than those reinforced every time. That is, they will continue without being reinforced. The effects of variable-ratio-reinforcement schedules on behavior have often been cited to explain why burglars, who are only sometimes successful (intermittent reinforcement), are more likely to return to the crime after being arrested, whereas perpetrators of fraud, who are closer to 100 percent successful, recidivate less often after being caught.

Personal characteristics. Criminal thinking and criminal action can also be characterized without direct reference to theory. Yochelson and Samenow (1976) have noted a variety of criminal traits. In varying degrees and combinations, one can observe these characteristics in the fraudulent offender. Our own research has confirmed the following traits.

Anger—Whether hidden in the "overcontrolled" person, or seen spilling over in the "undercontrolled" individual, anger does it's damage. The emotion of anger will crowd its owner to "get even." Anger spreads and spreads, eventually dominating feelings and thinking. Irrational acts are inevitable. Reason is replaced by "acting out," which also alleviates boredom. Excitement prevails. When anger is intense, caution is thrown to the wind and damage to persons or property results. In a less intense but chronic anger, a more calculated approach to inflicting damage is seen in the form of embezzlement and fraud. "They owe it to me. I earned it. It is their fault." Personal integrity may be compromised when anger or resentment peaks.

Pride—The particular brand of pride seen in the white-collar offender is the idea that he is better than others, more deserving, and "above" the rules that govern the general population. This extraordinary self-evaluation dominates his thinking so that he is discontented with any ordinary job or income. This distorted and unearned pride can be manifest in his mode of travel, dress, eating preferences, and life-style. Extending himself beyond his means is not unusual. The outward signs of success become an obsession. His "high-flying" tendencies may intrigue others as well, who want to go along for the ride. In some fraud-inclined individuals, pride may not be visible; a modest front is maintained while scheming toward their moment of triumph. In any event, there is an unyielding quality to their stance. This superior attitude causes the offender to often miscalculate or take chances seen by others as too risky. Pride blinds them to possible consequences, and their defective conscience frees them from the restraint of guilt. An offender may easily conclude that personal integrity can be upheld only by maintaining his pride and assumptions.

Power—For some individuals, power becomes the essence of self-worth. Money symbolizes power and therefore may preoccupy the mind of one who is determined to be "somebody." Other avenues to power, position, or prestige may be perceived as blocked, but the possibility of acquiring wealth is open. Power for the white-collar offender may lie in his or her ability to scheme, to beat the system, to outsmart the computer, or to outwit the powers that be. The idea of control is important to the offender. To be in charge, to make decisions, and to call the shots are important aspects for the power-oriented ego. Fantasies of influence dominate; dreams of unlimited freedom and complete control over his or her life motivate the white-collar criminal. Perhaps, on a more modest level, other fraud offenders simply want to get out from under the control of others. The power motive is strong and may surpass considerations of right or wrong.

Impatience—Delay of gratification has been viewed as evidence of a mature personality. In this sense, our white-collar offenders are often characterized as immature and unable to tolerate delay or frustration. The short-cut is quickly spotted. Failure in legitimate efforts simply stimulates a more earnest search for illegitimate routes to success in such personalities. It is unthinkable to continue on a course that is slow, plodding, and lacking a guarantee. To begin at the bottom and work up or to start over is just too much to ask. The temptation of easy gain or instant success is more than the offender can resist. In a sense, it is congruent for the immature, impatient personality to seek the more speedy route of fraud or embezzlement than to struggle in a conforming, lack-lustre manner. Planning ahead, with the prospects of hard work and trusting in oneself and others, is foreign to the offender. When crises occur or panic sets in, and fraud or embezzlement appears to be the answer, the offender is often unable to conceptualize alternatives or trust to legal recourse in solving problems. His predisposition is to resolve the financial problems immediately, in any way he can, with minimal effort and cost, no matter what the impact on the business or other persons might be. The approach is truly selfish.

The list could be extended, but these aspects appeal to us as central traits in typical white-collar offenders. Fraud is a multi-faceted phenomenon with common elements and yet unique characteristics in each case. Behavioral predispositions, thought patterns, needs, situations, and personal relationships must be considered in understanding the offender, in working with him, and in preventing fraudulent activities. Further empirical evidence will be required to evaluate these traits and theories of crime and fraud.

Discussion. Some psychological theories (dynamic theories) emphasize factors within the person, such as the center of behavior control. They point to response predispositions and personality consistencies in accounting for human actions. In contrast, other psychological explanations, especially learning theory, focus on the environment in identifying the locus of control. The assumptions in the latter case are that reinforcing and punishing contingencies in the environment operate as the critical elements in influencing behavior. It seems only logical to consider *both* internal and external factors in trying to understand a phenomenon such as fraud. A comprehensive psychological profile of the fraud-perpetrator and his crimes will have to use components of both internal variables and external variables; to ignore either makes for an incomplete explanation.

There is an obvious overlap between the psychological and sociological approaches. Sociology has traditionally been more active in developing theories of criminology and in explaining crime. Valuable insights and observations have come from a number of sources, suggesting that an interdisciplinary approach is essential to capturing all relevant data and ideas in order to explain criminal behavior.

Sociological Explanations of Crime

Several general theories have been proposed to explain why crime rates are higher among certain cultures, geographic regions, or races. These theories generally focus on some form of social disorganization.

Social disorganization. French sociologist Durkheim (1858-1917) first proposed the concept of "anomie," which refers to a condition of normlessness and social disruption when traditional rules lose their authority over behavior (Gibbons, 1973). The concept of anomie was first used by Durkheim to explain suicide rates. Others have elaborated on the concept of anomie to explain why crime rates are so high in minority and lower-class neighborhoods. Some have suggested that American society is anomic, since it places so much emphasis on success goals and status attainment, while the path to success is uncertain and blocked for many. Therefore, deviant behavior is to be found more frequently in places where individuals have greater difficulty achieving success, especially in lower-class areas.

The theory of social disorganization has enjoyed a fair degree of popularity in the field of sociology. Nevertheless, its usefulness is limited because of its generality. It fails to explain specific forms of deviation, and its general formulation does not permit specific tests of its propositions. Further, it is not aimed at the phenomenon of fraud, which is seen as a white-collar crime, a phenomenon of the middle and upper classes.

Differential association. One of the most well-known sociological explanations of criminal behavior is the theory of "differential association" first formulated by Sutherland (Sutherland and Cressey, 1978). This theory was first proposed to explain white-collar crime and is still considered by many to be the best explanation of white-collar crime.

In 1939, Sutherland coined the term "white-collar crime" in an address to the American Sociological Society. His influence has been both praised and criticized. While he stimulated thought and activity in white-collar crime research, he also provided confusion and inconsistency through his definitions and pronouncements. But Sutherland's interest was in refuting current theories, which then attributed criminal motivation to poverty and its concomitants.

In Sutherland's view, criminal behavior was linked to a person's association with a criminal environment. People encounter various social influences through their lifetimes. Some individuals encounter social interactions with carriers of criminalistic norms and become criminals as a consequence of this association. This process was called "differential association."

The elements in Sutherland's differential association theory can be summarized as follows (Sutherland and Cressey, 1978):

1. Criminal behavior is learned. It is not inherited, and the person who is not already trained in crime does not invent criminal behavior.

2. Criminal behavior is learned through interaction with other people in a process of both verbal and nonverbal communication.

3. The principle learning of criminal behavior occurs with intimate personal groups.

4. The learning of crime includes learning the techniques of committing the crime, along with the motives, drives, rationalizations, and attitudes that accompany it.

5. The specific direction of motives and drives is learned from definitions of the legal codes as favorable or unfavorable to violation. Sutherland said that in American society, these definitions are almost always mixed, with the consequence that we have cultural conflict regarding legal codes.

6. A person becomes delinquent because of an excess of definitions (or personal reactions) favorable to violating the law over definitions unfavorable to violating the law.

7. Differential associations may vary in frequency, duration, priority, and intensity. "Priority" refers to behavior

learned early in life, and is assumed to be important in the sense that lawful behavior developed in early childhood is likely to persist throughout life. "Intensity" is not precisely defined, but it has to do with such things as the prestige of the source of a criminal or anti-criminal pattern, and with emotional reactions related to the associations.

8. The process of learning criminal behavior by association with criminal patterns involves all of the mechanisms present in any other learning, including vicarious learning and imitation.

9. While criminal behavior is an expression of general needs and values, it is not explained by those general needs and values since non-criminal behavior is an expression of the same needs and values.

The essence of Sutherland's argument is that criminal behavior is enacted by individuals who have acquired a number of sentiments in favor of law violation that are sufficient to outweigh their pro-social or anti-criminal conduct definitions. Criminal behavior is learned from other criminals and will occur when the perceived rewards for criminal behavior exceed the rewards of lawful behavior. In general, contacts or associations with the greatest impact on persons are those that are frequent, lengthy, early in point of origin, and intense or meaningful.

The major criticism of the theory is that, like most sociological expositions, it lacks clarity and precision. It is not that its propositions are false, but that they are overly ambiguous; the propositions are plausible, but difficult to test. As a general theory explaining all criminal behavior, however, differential association is considered inadequate. Recently, several attempts have been undertaken to make differential association more specific and testable (DeFleur and Quinney, 1966; Cressey, 1966). Others have attempted to show how it is an application of modern learning theory based on principles of operant conditioning (Burgess and Akers, 1966; Jefferey, 1965). Actually, many elements of social learning theory and classical conditioning can be related to the notions of differential association. One of the most useful implications of differential association is the critical need for leaders and associates within an organization to be rigorously honest.

Cressey's non-sharable problem. A related, but alternative sociological theory of white-collar crime was proposed by Cressey (1953). He defined the problem as a "violation of a position of financial trust" that the person originally took in good faith. To quote from this work:

> Trusted persons become trust violators when they conceive of themselves as having a financial problem which is nonsharable, are aware that this problem can be secretly resolved by violation of the position of financial trust, and are able to apply to conduct in that situation verbalizations which enable them to adjust their conceptions of themselves as users of the entrusted funds or property.

Akers (1973) indicated that the entire process must be intact. There must be (a) a nonsharable problem, (b) an opportunity for trust violation, and (c) a set of rationalizations that define the behavior as appropriate in a given situation. None of these elements alone would be sufficient to result in embezzlement. Evidence for Cressey's theory rested on in-depth interviews with people convicted of trust violations. He claimed that all of the cases studied conformed to the three-step process, with no contradictory cases.

It would appear, from Cressey's extensive case-study analysis, that trust violation does not occur in the absence of the three steps. However, as Akers (1973) noted, it may be that trust violation does not always occur in the presence of the three steps. Nettler (1974) found that only one of six embezzlers fits Cressey's model. Also, it would be more convincing if independent and separate cross-validation studies confirmed the Cressey findings. Another problem with this model is using it, in its present form, to predict fraud. As an after-the-fact explanation it does well, but can the nonsharable problem and verbalizations be identified early enough to anticipate or predict a violation? The primary value of Cressey's work is the delineation of major variables that should be considered in a study of fraud.

Discussion. We believe that no single theory can adequately explain fraud and other criminal action. Gibbons (1973) claimed that the situation of criminology was similar to that of medicine: there is not one form of sickness, there are many. Furthermore, there is not just a single cause of illness; there are a number of causes, each related to a particular form of sickness. In criminology, therefore, fraud must be examined as a separate case in which the causes of fraud and its perpetrators are possibly different from those of other crimes. It is also probable that various types of fraud have different causes and are perpetrated by many kinds of people. This conclusion is supported by our own empirical comparison of fraud perpetrators with other criminals convicted of property offenses (see Appendix C).

* KEY POINTS *

* While perpetrators of fraud are criminal in their acts, they do not necessarily share traits with other types of criminals.
* Physiological traits do not appear related to fraud, but important research is continuing.
* Psychological disorders may be associated with crimes such as fraud, but most of those committing fraud are not mentally disturbed or considered psychologically abnormal.
* Both internal factors (personality) and external factors (environment) are likely to be important in explaining and predicting fraud.
* "Differential Association" emphasizes the fact that fraudulent behavior is learned by association with others who are dishonest and because of isolation from conforming persons.
* Cressey suggests the critical elements found in white-collar crime are
    a) a nonsharable problem
    b) an opportunity for trust violation,
    c) a set of rationalizations.
* Personal characteristics of offenders include anger, pride, power, and impatience.
* An integration or synthesis of ideas is needed to explain fraud.

APPENDIX B
RESEARCH
OBJECTIVES
AND METHODOLOGY

The research on which this book is based was funded by a grant from Peat, Marwick, Mitchell & Co. The original study had the following objectives:

1) To conduct an extensive review of all fraud-related literature

2) To identify the individual, organizational, and societal factors that suggest a high probability of fraud

3) To partially validate these factors by comparing them to past cases of fraud

4) To organize these factors into an early-warning system that can be used by auditors and managers in detecting and deterring fraud.

Underlying these objectives was the feeling that an understanding of fraud can only be achieved through a comprehensive study performed by an interdisciplinary team of researchers. Accordingly, the research team included individuals with backgrounds in accounting, information systems, organizational behavior, psychology, and criminology.

Review of the Literature and Other Sources

To accomplish the first research objective, the following four data sources were investigated: (1) literature citations, (2) fraud perpetrators and victims, (3) organizations concerned with fraud, and (4) legal and organizational documents. In conducting the literature review, over 1,500 fraud-related references were reviewed. These included books, journal and magazine articles, monographs, newspaper citations, and unpublished working papers (see Bibliography). With respect to the second data source, a number of perpetrators and victims of fraud were personally interviewed. These included representatives from both large and small corporations, members of auditing firms, and both parolled and incarcerated perpetrators of fraud.

Numerous organizations that are concerned with understanding either the detection, deterrence, prosecution or punishment of fraud were contacted. In many cases, these contacts included interviews with key people and reviews of internal documents. The following is a list of the data sources that were personally visited or examined by our project participants.

1. Comptroller of Currency
2. Major CPA firms, including seven of the "Big 8"
3. Department of Commerce
4. Department of the Treasury
5. FBI
6. Federal Reserve Board
7. National District Attorneys' Association
8. Pinkerton's (Investigative Agency)
9. Securities and Exchange Commission
10. Utah State Prison

Data was also gathered by mail and by telephone. A partial list of those contacted by letter and/or telephone includes:

1. Aetna Life and Casualty
2. American Bankers' Association
3. American Bar Association
4. American Institute of Certified Public Accountants
5. Apex Charitable Trust
6. Automation Training Center
7. Bank Administration Institute
8. Battelle Institute
9. U.S. Chamber of Commerce
10. Commercial Union Assurance Corporation
11. Computerworld
12. Continental Insurance Co.

13. Crum and Forster
14. Department of Housing and Urban Development
15. Department of Justice
16. Department of the Treasury
17. Every prison in the U.S. and Canada with a population of over 400 inmates
18. Every women's prison in the U.S. and Canada with a population of over 100 inmates
19. Federal Deposit Insurance Corp.
20. Federal Trade Commission
21. Fidelity and Deposit Co. of Maryland
22. Fireman's Fund Insurance Co.
23. Government of Japan, Ministry of Justice
24. Hartford Insurance Co.
25. IBM Corporation
26. INA Corporation
27. Insight Services (a private detective firm)
28. Institute of Internal Auditors
29. Internal Revenue Service
30. International Association of Chiefs of Police
31. International Criminal Police Organization
32. Library Centre of Criminology, Toronto, Canada
33. Lloyds of London
34. Ministry of the Solicitor General, Research Division, Ottawa, Canada
35. National Association of Attorney Generals
36. National Council on Crime and Delinquency
37. National Criminal Justice Reference Service
38. National Institute of Law Enforcement and Criminal Justice (LEAA)
39. Office of Management and Budget
40. Personnel Security Corporation
41. Public Information Officer, Federal Bureau of Prisons
42. Reid Associates
43. Reliance Insurance Co.

44. Research Departments of State Divisions of Corrections
45. Research Unit, U.S. Parole Commission
46. St. Paul Fire and Marine Insurance Company
47. State Parole Departments
48. State Probation Departments
49. The Surety Association of America
50. TransAmerica Corporation
51. United Nations Asia and Far East Institute for the Prevention of Crime
52. United Nations Social Defense Research Institute
53. United Pacific Insurance Co.
54. U.S. Fidelity and Guarantee Co.
55. Yale University Fraud Study Group

The fourth data source, and certainly one of the most helpful, was the examination of legal and organizational documents. Donn Parker's extensive files, containing over 400 documented computer-fraud cases, were examined in detail. In addition, numerous probation, parole, and prison records provided significant insights into the characteristics of fraud perpetrators.

Identification of Individual, Organizational, and Societal Factors

As the data sources were examined, a comprehensive list of all variables that appeared to influence or be associated with the perpetration of fraud was compiled. The variables identified in this listing were classified into three major categories: societal (see Chapter 10), organizational (see Chapters 3-5), and individual factors (see Chapters 7-9). Once identified, they were content and factor analyzed. During this process, patterns and relationships among the variables emerged and a tentative model explaining fraud was developed.

Validation of Fraud-Related Variables

To partially validate the fraud-related variables identified in step two, 52 cases of alleged fraud were studied.

For these cases, an extensive search was conducted to identify all published accounts of the fraud. The 52 cases are:

1. Allied Crude Vegetable Oil Co.
2. Ampex
3. Baltimore Federal Credit vs. U.S.
4. Barchris
5. Beardsley vs. Ernst
6. Beverly Hills Bankcorp
7. Bille Sol Estes
8. Black Watch Farms, Inc.
9. Cenco
10. CIT Financial
11. Cobuild
12. Continental Vending
13. Cosmopolitan Investors Funding
14. Craig vs. Angon
15. Croissant vs. Watrud
16. Equity Funding
17. Essley Shirt Co.
18. Firestone Group Ltd.
19. Fisco
20. Four Seasons
21. Georgia Pacific
22. Geotek
23. Giant Stores
24. G. L. Miller
25. Hochfelder
26. Homestake Production
27. Koscot-Glenn Turner
28. Lutz vs. First Security Bank
29. McKesson Robbins
30. National Student Marketing

31. Omega-Alpha, Inc.
32. Penn Central
33. Photon, Inc.
34. Republic National Life
35. Rhode Island Hospital Trust National Bank
36. R. Hoe & Co.
37. S. J. Minerals
38. Smith et. al. vs. London Assurance
39. State Street Trust vs. Ernst
40. Stephens Industries
41. Stirling Homex
42. Talley Industries
43. Ultramares
44. United Brands
45. U.S. vs. Benjamin
46. Vesco
47. Westec
48. Western Properties
49. Westgate-U.S. Financial
50. Wheatheart Cattle Co.
51. Whitacker Corp.
52. Yale Express

Each case was carefully analyzed to determine which of the items on the master list appeared to be present in the case. At the completion of this process, each item on the master list was carefully reviewed and the master list revised.

In revising the master list, only those variables that could be associated with at least one case were kept. This is a somewhat demanding criterion because certainly the authors who wrote about the cases had a perspective much different from ours.

Development of an Early-Warning System for Fraud

After completing the compilation and validation steps, a fraud checklist for use by auditors was developed (see Chapter

6). This checklist, which includes questions auditors will ask themselves about the client and that the client will ask about themselves, should make auditors more aware of the possibility of fraud and hence increase the probability that fraud will be detected. The checklist includes factors that would motivate an employee to commit fraud for his own benefit against a company, and that would motivate an executive to commit fraud on behalf of a corporation.

APPENDIX C
COMPARATIVE CHARACTERISTICS OF FRAUD PERPETRATORS: AN EMPIRICAL ANALYSIS

This Appendix Explains:

- The difficulty in conducting empirical studies on fraud.
- Demographic, psychological, and criminal differences between fraud perpetrators and other property offenders.
- Psychological differences between fraud perpetrators and noncriminals.
- Demographic, psychological, and criminal differences between fraud perpetrators who have been imprisoned and those sentenced to probation.

Most articles and books on fraud are either theoretical or narrative descriptions of particular cases. Few studies empirically describe fraud perpetrators as a group or differentiate between them and other groups. A major difficulty in conducting such studies is the small percentage of criminals identifiable as "fraud perpetrators." Criminals who might be labeled "fraud perpetrators" have usually been convicted of crimes such as grand larceny, forgery, stolen property, etc. In addition, fraud perpetrators comprise only a small percentage of all incarcerated federal prisoners. In 1975, only 527 of the 20,949 federal inmates had been convicted of embezzlement or fraud, according to a letter received from the Bureau of Prisons, United States Department of Justice (Lebowitz, 1978). The Texas Department of Corrections stated that of 17,868 total inmates in 1975, only 24 were incarcerated for embezzlement (Hayes, 1978).

Because of the lack of descriptive empirical studies concerning fraud perpetrators, the authors decided to do some preliminary research of their own. The research question was whether fraud perpetrators, as a group, are different from the normal population and whether they are different from other criminals. Another important question to be answered was whether there are different kinds of fraud perpetrators. To begin to answer these questions, it was decided to compare incarcerated fraud perpetrators with (1) other incarcerated property offenders, (2) normal persons, and (3) fraud offenders on probation. Fraud perpetrators were defined for purposes of this study as those who were in managerial or professional positions and who illegally appropriated thousands of dollars from their employers. Utah State Prison's computerized records for the past five years were searched, and 23 fraud perpetrators who fit this definition were identified. These 23 prisoners were compared with all other property offenders from the same time period on whom all of the necessary information was available. Some of their files had missing data, so the numbers analyzed on different traits were not always the same.

Most criminologists would agree that incarcerated fraud perpetrators are, in all probability, not typical of fraud perpetrators generally. When compared to other criminals, fraud perpetrators are less likely to be caught, turned in, arrested, convicted, incarcerated, or made to serve long sentences. Therefore, only those with the most severe crimes and most extensive criminal records are likely to be sent to prison. This should be kept in mind when trying to apply findings to nonincarcerated offenders.

COMPARISON WITH OTHER PROPERTY OFFENDERS

The fraud perpetrators were compared with the other property offenders on demographic, criminal, and personality variables to determine if there were significant differences between the two groups. Means (averages) and standard deviations were calculated on all continuous variables, and comparisons were calculated using t-tests to determine if there were significant differences between means obtained by the two groups on each of the continuous variables. On dichotomous variables, proportions were computed on all traits for each group, and Z-tests of the difference of two proportions were calculated to determine if there were significant differences between the fraud perpetrators and the other property offenders. The results of these analyses are presented in Tables C-1, C-2, and C-3.

Many differences were found between the two groups. Some were noted in their physical descriptions. The larger percentage of Spanish-Americans is probably unique to the sample, since six of the seven were convicted in one incident. The fraud perpetrators were considerably older, the average being born in 1931, compared to the average year of birth of 1948 for the property offenders. Since the inmates were incarcerated during different years, no definite age at incarceration can be determined, but it would be approximately 44 and 27 years old, respectively for the average years of 1931 and 1948. The older age of the fraud perpetrators might be expected, since it usually takes longer to get into managerial positions or other positions of trust. Possibly because of the age difference, and in spite of the larger percentage of women, the fraud perpetrators were about 23 pounds heavier. Whereas only 2 percent of the property offenders were female, 30 percent of the fraud perpetrators were women. A high percentage of women among fraud perpetrators was also found by Simon (1978), head of the University of Illinois program on Law and Society. She reported that between 1953 and 1975, the proportion of women charged with embezzlement and fraud jumped 300 percent. According to Simon, as women increasingly obtain jobs in positions of trust that allow them to steal and embezzle, these rates will continue to rise. Another physical difference is that the fraud perpetrator is much less likely to have been tattooed. Part of this difference is probably due to the higher incidence of women among this group, but this could account for only part of the difference. It is important to note that many authors have found a relationship between being tattooed and criminality (Taylor, 1968, 1970; Lander and Kohn, 1967). Burma (1959) stated that about 10 percent of the normal population is tattooed, which is very similar to the 13 percent of fraud perpetrators found in this study.

The fact that the fraud perpetrators are older possibly ex-

Table C-1

Differences of Proportions Between
Fraud Perpetrators and Other Property Offenders

Traits	Fraud Perpetrators (N=23)		Property Offenders (N=677)		Z-Test of Diff.	Level of Significance**
	Number Having Trait	Percent Having Trait	Number Having Trait	Percent Having Trait		
State of Residence						
Utah	18	78	553	83	−.58	ns
Pacific	3	13	33	5	1.72	ns
Mountain	2	9	27	4	1.09	ns
Central	0	0	35	5	−1.13	ns
Eastern	0	0	12	2	−.65	ns
Non U.S.	0	0	7	1	−.49	ns
Male	16	70	651	98	−7.36	.001
Race						
Caucasian	16	70	517	78	−.89	ns
Spanish-American	7	30	86	13	2.42	.05
American-Indian	0	0	10	2	−.59	ns
Black	0	0	53	8	−1.41	ns
Marital Status						
Married	16	70	215	32	3.73	.001
Single	7	30	306	46	−1.46	ns
Divorced	0	0	143	21	−2.46	.05
Injury to Person	0	0	47	7	−1.32	ns
Weapon Used	0	0	182	27	−2.92	.01
Drug-Related Crime	0	0	213	32	−3.26	.001
Alcohol-Related Crime	2	9	242	36	−2.72	.01
Plead Guilty	16	70	525	78	−1.05	ns
Drug User	2	9	515	77	−7.45	.001
Alcohol User	17	74	599	90	−2.42	.05
Tattooed	3	13	406	61	−4.59	.001
Religion						
Mormon	15	65	250	37	2.69	.01
Catholic	5	22	164	25	−.31	ns
Protestant	2	9	92	13	−.70	ns
Other	1	4	65	10	−.87	ns
None	0	0	96	14	−1.96	.05

228

Table C-1 (cont'd.)

Differences of Proportions Between
Fraud Perpetrators and Other Property Offenders

Traits	Fraud Perpetrators (N=23)		Property Offenders (N=677)		Z-Test of Diff.	Level of Signifi-cance**
	Number Having Trait	Percent Having Trait	Number Having Trait	Percent Having Trait		
*Been in Mental Hospital	3	14	169	25	−1.25	ns
*Been in Juvenile Institution	1	5	315	47	−3.95	.001
*Escaped from Prison or Jail	1	5	186	28	−2.42	.05
*Absconded from Proba-tion or Parole	4	18	210	31	−1.33	ns
*Runaway from Juvenile Institution	0	0	160	24	−2.62	.01
Lived with Parents at Age 14						
Both	15	65	316	47	1.68	ns
Mother Only	5	22	213	32	−1.03	ns
Father Only	1	4	22	3	.27	ns
Neither	2	9	116	17	−1.09	ns
Previously on Probation	9	39	517	77	−4.25	.001
Previously on Parole	5	22	260	39	−1.67	ns

*N=22

**.05, .01, .001 means that differences this great could happen by chance in 5 chances out of 100, 1 chance out of 100, and 1 chance out of 1000 respectively (ns represents nonsignificant)

Table C-2

Differences of Means Between
Fraud Perpetrators and Other Property Offenders v

Traits	Fraud Perpetrators			Property Offenders			t-Test of Difference	Signifi- cance Level
	Number	Mean	Standard Deviation	Number	Mean	Standard Deviation		
Year Born	23	1931.70	6.55	667	1948.53	8.14	−11.76	.001
Height in Inches	23	69.04	3.55	667	69.91	3.20	−1.20	ns
Weight	23	182.74	41.50	667	159.91	24.17	2.48	.05
Number of Children	22	2.55	.86	667	1.10	1.55	7.36	.001
Education Completed	23	13.55	2.40	667	10.56	1.81	5.40	.001
Rap Sheet Entries	22	8.36	8.27	667	12.07	11.43	−3.29	.001
Age at First Arrest	22	30.59	10.36	667	16.23	5.20	6.33	.001
No. of Sentences Served	22	1.85	1.90	667	1.80	1.28	.12	ns
I.Q.	21	108.71	18.71	667	100.18	15.79	1.87	ns
Tested Grade Level	16	9.19	1.94	667	8.58	1.65	1.21	ns

Table C-3

Differences of Bipolar Scores Between Fraud Perpetrators and Other Property Offenders

Test Scales	Fraud Perpetrators (N=19)		Property Offenders (N=677)		t-Test of Differences	Significance Level
	Mean	Standard Deviation	Mean	Standard Deviation		
Invalid	.05	.23	.36	.98	−4.70	.001
Lie	6.37	3.89	5.60	2.85	.83	ns
Defensive	8.68	3.33	9.67	3.95	−1.24	ns
Psychic Pain	8.00	4.28	8.68	4.70	−.66	ns
Depression	5.10	3.33	8.01	4.40	−3.62	.001
Self-Degradation	3.26	3.41	5.42	4.20	−2.63	.01
Dependence	3.37	2.69	5.92	3.81	−3.92	.001
Unmotivated	3.32	2.67	6.30	3.18	−4.65	.001
Social Withdrawal	6.21	4.78	7.64	4.89	−1.25	ns
Family Discord	3.53	4.55	6.88	5.22	−3.07	.01
Sexual Immaturity	3.68	2.11	4.61	3.43	−1.80	ns
Social Deviancy	6.95	4.24	11.32	3.61	−4.33	.001
Impulsiveness	6.42	4.14	8.81	4.76	−2.41	.05
Hostility	3.32	3.00	6.08	4.00	−3.81	.001
Insensitivity	3.00	1.89	5.87	3.01	−6.23	.001

plains why more of them were married and why they had more children than other criminals. In the case of the property offenders, 21 percent were divorced, as compared to no divorces among the fraud perpetrators. This, in conjunction with the lower average score on the Bipolar's Family Discord scale, would indicate that the fraud perpetrators have a much more stable family situation.

Social Differences

There were many social differences between the groups. It was found that, as a group, the fraud perpetrators had gone to school about three years longer. They were less likely to use alcohol and considerably less likely to use drugs. This latter fact is possibly due to the younger generation's greater acceptance of drugs. A higher proportion of the fraud perpetrators were Mormons (the predominant religion in Utah), whereas more of the property offenders professed no religion.

The criminal backgrounds of the two groups also proved significantly different. The FBI's rap sheet of criminal bookings showed fewer entries for the fraud perpetrators, about eight, compared to about twelve for the other property offenders. It is interesting that the fraud perpetrators had this many entries on their rap sheets. It might be hypothesized that this is why these particular fraud perpetrators were incarcerated, while others with a shorter criminal record were placed on probation. On all other criminal background traits that significantly differentiated between the two groups, the other property offenders were found to be more criminal. The property offenders were found to start their criminal careers at a younger age, and were more likely to have been sent to juvenile correctional institutions. In addition, the other property offenders were more likely to have escaped from a jail or prison, or to have run away from a juvenile institution. A larger percentage of them had also been placed on probation. Consistent with the kind of crime committed by the two groups, the property offenders had a higher probability of using a weapon in the commission of their crimes, and their crimes were also more alcohol- or drug-related.

Besides coming out comparatively better on many descriptive traits, fraud perpetrators have been determined by the U.S. Bureau of Prisons Office of Research to have an excellent record of success on parole. For those convicted of tax embezzlement crimes, 95.4 percent were successful in staying out of prison after two years (Prather, 1977), a much higher rate than for offenders in general.

Psychological Differences

Differences between the fraud and property offender groups were also found on psychological traits, as measured by the Bipolar Psychological Inventory (Howell, Payne, and Roe, 1972), a personality test designed specifically for use with criminal populations (See Table 3). The other property offenders were found more likely to invalidate their tests by not being able to read the answers, by being careless, or by making obviously absurd answers. This is possibly a result of their poorer academic skills. On all of the personality variables in which there were significant differences, the fraud perpetrators' scores indicated that they were in better psychological health. They had more optimism, self-esteem, self-sufficiency, achievement motivation, and family harmony in contrast to the other property offenders who showed more depression, self-degradation, dependence, lack of motivation, and family discord. The Bipolar's criminal or character disorder scales also found the fraud perpetrators to have significantly fewer problems. They expressed more social conformity, self control, kindness, and empathy when compared to the other property offenders' greater social deviancy, impulsiveness, hostility, and insensitivity to other people.

COMPARISON WITH NONCRIMINALS

The Bipolar Psychological Inventory test scores of the incarcerated fraud perpetrators were also compared to the scores of a sample of college students. As can be seen in Table C-4, it was found that there were only six scales that significantly differentiated the criminals from the college students. On three of the scales (Lie, Psychic Pain, and Social Deviancy) the fraud perpetrators scored more pathologically than the students. However, the students scored lower on the Dependence, Sexual Immaturity, and Insensitivity scales. These comparisons showed that the fraud perpetrators' personality scores were more similar to those of the students than to those of other property offenders.

These comparisons indicated that incarcerated fraud perpetrators looked considerably "better" than criminals committing other property offenses and were more similar to college students.

Table C-4

Differences of Bipolar Scores Between Fraud Perpetrators and College Students

Test Scales	Fraud Perpetrators (N=19)		Students (N=148)		t-Test of Differences	Significance Level
	Mean	Standard Deviation	Mean	Standard Deviation		
Invalid	.05	.23	.15	.39	−1.59	ns
Lie	6.37	3.89	4.34	2.26	2.17	.05
Defensiveness	8.68	3.33	7.74	3.55	1.12	ns
Psychic Pain	8.00	4.28	5.11	3.04	2.78	.01
Depression	5.10	3.33	3.70	2.65	1.72	ns
Self-Degra-dation	3.26	3.41	2.92	2.52	0.41	ns
Dependence	3.37	2.69	5.61	5.64	−2.81	.01
Unmotivated	3.32	2.67	4.09	2.49	−1.16	ns
Social With-drawal	6.21	4.78	5.26	4.17	.81	ns
Family Discord	3.53	4.55	4.59	3.54	−0.95	ns
Sexual Immaturity	3.68	2.11	5.26	3.03	−2.84	.01
Social Deviancy	6.95	4.24	3.77	2.53	3.11	.05
Impulsiveness	6.42	4.14	8.59	4.09	−1.71	ns
Hostility	3.32	3.00	3.59	2.67	−0.36	ns
Insensitivity	3.00	1.89	6.16	2.89	−6.25	.001

COMPARISON OF PRISONERS AND PROBATIONERS

Comparisons between incarcerated and probationed fraud perpetrators are given in Tables C-5 and C-6. There were few differences between the two groups. The probable reason for the significantly higher percentage of Spanish-Americans has already been noted. There was no apparent explanation for the higher percentage of individuals who were divorced or of those professing no religion among the probationers, or of the higher percentage of Catholics among the incarcerated. However, a partial explanation for why individuals of one group were incarcerated while the other given probation was found in the three comparisons with the most significant differences. The incarcerated group was an average of about 12 years

Table C-5

Differences of Proportions Between
Incarcerated and Probationer Fraud Perpetrators

Traits	Incarcerated			Probationer			Z-Test of Difference	Significance Level
	Number Having Trait	Number in Sample	Percentage Having Trait	Number Having Trait	Number in Sample	Percentage Having Trait		
State of Residence								
Utah	18	23	78	18	20	90	1.04	ns
Pacific	3	23	13	0	20	0	1.67	ns
Mountain	2	23	9	2	20	10	−.15	ns
Male	16	23	70	13	21	62	.54	ns
Race								
Caucasian	16	23	70	21	21	100	−2.76	.01
Spanish-American	7	23	30	0	21	0	2.76	.01
Marital Status								
Married	16	23	70	13	21	62	.54	ns
Single	7	23	30	3	21	14	1.28	ns
Divorced	0	23	00	5	21	24	−2.49	.05
Drug-Related Crime	0	23	0	0	18	0	0	ns
Alcohol-Related Crime	2	23	9	1	18	6	−1.14	ns
Plead Guilty	16	23	70	18	21	86	−1.28	ns
Drug User	2	23	9	1	15	7	.23	ns
Alcohol User	17	23	74	3	15	20	3.25	.001
Tattooed	3	23	13	0	17	0	1.54	ns

Table C-5 (cont'd.)

Differences of Proportions Between
Incarcerated and Probationer Fraud Perpetrators

Traits	Incarcerated			Probationer			Z-Test of Difference	Significance Level
	Number Having Trait	Number in Sample	Percentage Having Trait	Number Having Trait	Number in Sample	Percentage Having Trait		
Religion								
Mormon	15	23	65	12	17	71	−.35	ns
Catholic	5	23	22	0	17	0	2.06	.05
Protestant	2	23	9	1	17	6	.33	ns
Other	1	23	4	0	17	0	.87	ns
None	0	23	0	4	17	24	−2.45	.05
Been in Mental Hospital	3	22	14	0	13	0	1.39	ns
Been in Juvenile Institution	1	22	5	0	13	0	.78	ns
Absconded	4	22	18	0	13	0	1.63	ns
Lived with Parents at Age 14								
Both	15	23	65	9	13	69	−.25	ns
Mother Only	5	23	22	1	13	08	1.09	ns
Father Only	1	23	4	1	13	08	−.42	ns
Neither	2	23	9	2	13	15	−.61	ns
Previous Probation	9	23	39	2	13	15	1.49	ns
Previous Parole	5	23	22	2	13	15	.46	ns

Table C-6

Differences of Means Between
Incarcerated and Probationer Fraud Perpetrators

Traits	Incarcerated			Probationer			t-Test of Difference	Significance Level
	Number	Mean	Standard Deviation	Number	Mean	Standard Deviation		
Year Born	23	1931.70	6.55	21	1943.67	6.91	−5.43	.001
Height in Inches	23	69.04	3.55	17	69.29	3.85	.20	ns
Weight	23	182.74	41.50	15	169.87	35.02	1.00	ns
No. of Children	22	2.55	.86	13	2.77	2.09	−.35	ns
Education Completed	23	13.55	2.40	17	13.76	1.82	−.31	ns
No. of Rap Sheet Entries	22	8.36	8.27	17	1.47	1.01	3.78	.001
Age at First Arrest	22	30.59	10.36	17	32.35	8.18	−.58	ns

older, had been arrested many more times, and had many more members who drank alcohol. Of the incarcerated group, 74 percent used alcohol, as compared to only 20 percent of the probationers. It can be seen that overall, the probationers had fewer problems than the incarcerated fraud perpetrators.

A NATIONAL SAMPLE OF FRAUD PERPETRATORS

An attempt was made to collect and analyze a national sample of fraud perpetrators to determine their characteristics and to do intercorrelations and a factor analysis of these characteristics. A letter requesting information similar to what was obtained for the Utah sample was sent to every male prison with 400 or more prisoners, every female prison with 100 or more prisoners, and to every state and federal probation and parole department in the United States and Canada. A total of 531 requests were sent, and only 64 agencies responded. Of these, 44 said they could not provide the data requested, and only 20 prisons sent the requested data on a total of 26 prisoners. Five of the most common reasons given for not complying with our request were: (a) they had no fraud perpetrators or none fitting our description, (b) fraud perpetrators could be listed under many different crime categories, (c) they had no personnel to search the records, (d) they had no computerized files, (e) it would take too much time, and (f) it might violate security or privacy laws. Thus, the data compiled on the 26 prisoners incarcerated for fraud hardly constitutes a "national sample."

Descriptive statistics of the sample including means, standard deviations, proportions, and comparisons with the Utah sample are presented in Tables C-7 and C-8. Because there were missing data on some responses from corrections agencies, the numbers analyzed vary on different traits. It is interesting to note that on 25 of the 30 comparisons, there were no significant differences between the national sample and the Utah fraud perpetrators. This would suggest that these were quite similar groups. Even though the national sample scored significantly higher on their tested grade level, their mean measured grade level of 10.72 (sophomore in high school) is very low for people in managerial or professional positions. It might be speculated that this low academic ability is one rea-

Table C-7

Differences of Means Between
Utah and National Samples of Fraud Perpetrators

Traits	Utah			National			t-Test of Difference	Significance Level
	Number	Mean	Standard Deviation	Number	Mean	Standard Deviation		
Year Born	23	1931.70	6.55	26	1934.23	7.96	−1.19	ns
Number of Children	22	2.55	.86	23	2.65	1.30	−.30	ns
Education Completed	23	13.55	2.40	26	13.38	2.98	.22	ns
No. of Rap Sheet Entries	22	8.36	8.27	19	5.37	12.70	.86	ns
Age at First Arrest	22	30.59	10.36	21	33.14	11.91	−.73	ns
No. of Sentences Served	22	1.85	1.90	24	1.38	1.01	1.01	ns
I.Q.	21	108.71	18.71	10	115.30	8.27	−1.32	ns
Tested Grade Level	16	9.19	1.94	12	10.72	1.51	−2.26	.05

Table C-8

Differences of Proportions Between
Utah and National Samples of Fraud Perpetrators

Traits	Utah			National			Z-Test of Difference	Significance Level
	Number Having Trait	Number in Sample	Percentage Having Trait	Number Having Trait	Number in Sample	Percentage Having Trait		
Race								
Caucasian	16	23	70	26	26	10	-3.04	.001
Spanish-American	7	23	30	0	26	0	2.04	.001
Marital Status								
Married	16	23	70	18	26	69	.03	ns
Single	7	23	30	1	26	4	2.51	.05
Divorced	0	23	0	7	26	27	-2.69	.01
Drug-Related Crime	0	23	0	7	26	27	-2.69	.01
Alcohol-Related Crime	2	23	9	2	24	8	-1.41	ns
Plead Guilty	16	23	70	15	25	60	.69	ns
Drug User	2	23	9	2	22	9	-.05	ns
Alcohol User	17	23	74	14	23	61	.94	ns
Tattooed	3	22	13	5	23	22	-.78	ns
Been in Mental Hospital	3	22	14	3	22	14	.00	ns
Been in Juvenile Institution	1	22	5	3	26	12	-.87	ns
Escaped from Jail or Prison	1	22	5	1	26	4	.12	ns

Table C-8 (cont'd.)

Differences of Proportions Between Utah and National Samples of Fraud Perpetrators

Traits	Utah			National			Z-Test of Difference	Significance Level
	Having Trait	Number in Sample	Percentage Having Trait	Number Having Trait	Number in Sample	Percentage Having Trait		
Absconded Parole or Probation	4	22	18	1	25	4	1.57	ns
Runaway from Juvenile Institution	0	22	0	2	25	8	−1.36	ns
Lived with Parents at Age 14								
Both	15	23	65	17	21	81	−1.17	ns
Mother Only	5	23	22	3	21	14	.64	ns
Father Only	1	23	04	1	21	5	−.07	ns
Neither	2	23	9	0	21	0	1.38	ns
Previously on Probation	9	23	39	7	22	32	.51	ns
Previously on Parole	5	23	22	1	20	5	1.58	ns

son that these particular fraud perpetrators committed the crime, got caught, and/or were convicted. In looking at individual fraud perpetrators in both the Utah and national samples, one interesting observation was made. In almost all cases, the individual either had many criminal traits and an extensive criminal background or was very clean as far as criminality was concerned. For instance, the group with the most criminal traits had committed an average of 15 crimes per person, the "clean" group had committed an average of only one and a half crimes per person. If this observation holds up in larger samples, it might be hypothesized that there are two distinct types of fraud perpetrators: (1) the chronic criminal type who engages in fraud as just another in a series of crimes, and (2) the more typical business person who succumbs to pressures or temptation. There is distinct similarity between these two types of fraud perpetrators and the two types of murderer (overcontrolled and undercontrolled) as hypothesized by Megargee (1966). According to Megargee, violence in the undercontrolled person is attributed to a lack of adequate controls. The overcontrolled individual has to build very high levels of the aggressive impulse to overcome his high inhibitions of aggression. The aggressive impulses do build up in this second group because they do not have alternative means of expressing their hostility. It would appear from observations of our analyzed groups that some fraud perpetrators are of the psychopathic, antisocial type who lack internal controls, who are hedonistic, and who do not learn from the consequences of their actions. Those in the undercontrolled group are likely to become involved in crime over and over again, and have long criminal records and criminal personalities. The overcontrolled type would be very moral, trustworthy, and have controls of a very high level. However, his need or desire to misappropriate company funds will continue to grow because his rigidity deprives him of alternative methods of meeting these needs. The first type will steal any time he has the chance; the second type will steal only when the level of desire overcomes the high level of control.

In summary, the results of the study indicated that incarcerated fraud perpetrators are more like the average population than they are like other criminals. These results help to explain why fraud perpetrators cannot be described by a criminal career profile.

APPENDIX D

FRAUD VALIDATION TABLES

Tables showing the validation of the red flag list with 52 cases of fraud.

Individuals on Behalf of the Company	Allied Crude Vegetable Oil	Ampex	Baltimore Fed. Credit	Barchris	Beardsley vs. Ernst	Beverly Hills Bankcorp	Bille Sol Estes	Black Watch Farms, Inc.	Cenco	CIT Financial	Cobuild	Continental Vending	Cosmopolitan Invst. Funding	Craig vs. Angon	Croissant vs. Watrud	Equity Funding	Essley Shirt Co.	Firestone Group Ltd.	Fisco
1. Heavy investments or losses	×	×		×		×						×	×			×			×
2. Insufficient working capital	×	×		×		×	×	×	×	×		×				×		×	
3. High debt	×	×		×	×	×	×	×	×	×		×				×			
4. Reduced credit		×		×		×				×		×							
5. Profit squeeze		×				×	×												
6. Restrictive agreements		×																	
7. Deteriorating earnings	×	×		×		×				×						×			
8. Urgent need for favorable earnings		×		×	×	×			×			×				×		×	
9. Temporarily bad situation		×		×		×			×	×						×			
10. Unmarketable collateral	×					×				×		×	×			×			
11. Corporate dependence	×			×		×			×	×								×	
12. Excess capacity	×																		
13. Severe obsolescence		×																	
14. Long business cycle		×		×						×									
15. Revoked or imperiled licenses	×																		
16. Rapid expansion	×	×		×	×	×	×	×	×	×						×			×
17. Unfavorable economic conditions	×	×		×		×										×			
18. Difficulty in collecting receivables				×		×					×	×							
19. Heavy competition	×	×		×															
20. Sales backlog		×																	
21. Pressure to merge																			
22. Inventory increase without sales increase																			
23. Significant tax adjustments	×											×							
24. Significant litigation	×			×												×			
25. Stock exchange suspension	×						×	×				×				×			
TOTAL	14	15	0	14	3	13	5	4	6	9	1	9	2	0	0	11	0	3	2

TABLE D-1
SITUATIONAL PRESSURE RED FLAGS: FRAUD FOR COMPANY BENEFIT

	Four Seasons	Georgia Pacific	Geotek	Giant Stores	G. L. Miller	Hochfelder	Homestake Production	Koscot—Glenn Turner	Lutz vs. First Sec. Bank	McKesson Robbins	Nat. Student Marketing	Omega-Alpha, Inc.	Penn Central	Photon, Inc.	Republic National Life	Rhode Is. Hosp. Trust	R. Hoe & Co.	S. J. Minerals	Smith vs. London Assurance	State Street Trust	Stephens Industries	Stirling Homex	Talley Industries	Ultramares	United Brands	U.S. vs. Benjamin	Vesco	Westec	Western Properties	Westgate—U.S. Financial	Wheatheart Cattle Co.	Whitaker Corp.	Yale Express	TOTAL
	×	×		×	×	×	×			×	×		×	×	×	×	×			×		×			×				×	×			×	26
	×			×		×	×			×	×		×	×		×	×			×		×			×			×		×			×	25
	×			×		×				×			×	×	×		×					×	×	×			×	×	×			×	×	26
	×			×			×			×			×	×		×	×			×										×	×		×	17
	×					×				×			×			×						×	×										×	11
							×								×	×						×												5
			×				×			×			×			×	×					×			×								×	14
	×			×			×	×		×	×		×	×	×	×				×		×	×			×			×		×	×	×	24
			×			×				×			×			×				×	×	×								×			×	16
													×						×			×			×							×		8
	×	×					×			×			×	×	×	×	×			×		×	×			×	×	×	×					20
													×		×																	×		4
										×			×	×						×		×												6
	×																			×		×										×		6
	×												×																					3
	×	×		×			×	×		×	×		×	×	×	×	×			×		×	×			×	×	×			×	×	×	31
	×			×						×			×		×	×	×			×		×				×			×		×		×	16
	×		×	×	×					×			×						×	×	×	×					×				×		×	17
	×			×									×			×				×				×							×		×	8
														×					×	×											×			4
		×	×	×						×			×			×						×				×			×		×		×	9
																																		0
	×	×				×							×				×																	5
	×	×				×	×			×			×		×		×	×												×				12
	×					×				×			×		×		×			×	×	×								×	×			15
16	5	1	12	2	3	9	3	0	10	9	0	15	8	12	10	12	4	0	7	2	16	9	1	3	5	1	8	4	7	6	1	13	

TABLE D-1 Cont'd.

Individuals on Behalf of the Company	Allied Crude Vegetable Oil	Ampex	Baltimore Fed. Credit	Barchris	Beardsley vs. Ernst	Beverly Hills Bankcorp	Bille Sol Estes	Black Watch Farms, Inc.	Cenco	CIT Financial	Cobuild	Continental Vending	Cosmopolitan Invst. Funding	Craig vs. Angon	Croissant vs. Watrud	Equity Funding	Essley Shirt Co.	Firestone Group Ltd.	Fisco
1. Related party transactions	×			×					×	×	×	×	×			×			
2. Complex business structure	×	×		×	×					×						×			
3. Ineffective internal auditing staff	×	×							×			×				×			×
4. Highly computerized firm									×							×			
5. Atypical or "hot" industry		×		×				×								×			
6. Several different auditing firms or changes auditors often					×			×				×				×			
7. Reluctance to give auditors data	×			×	×			×				×	×	×		×			
8. Several different legal firms or changes legal counsel often																			
9. Large number of banks	×			×	×					×		×				×			
10. Continuous problems with regulatory agencies	×							×								×			
11. Large year-end or unusual transactions		×		×	×			×	×		×	×				×		×	
12. Inadequate internal controls or nonenforcement of existing controls	×	×	×					×				×	×	×		×			×
13. Liberal accounting practices	×	×		×		×				×				×		×		×	×
14. Poor accounting records	×	×	×	×			×					×				×			
15. Inadequate staffing of accounting department	×	×	×																
16. Inadequate disclosures of unusual accounting practices	×			×		×		×	×	×	×	×				×		×	
TOTAL	11	8	3	9	5	2	1	7	5	5	3	9	3	3	0	14	0	3	3

TABLE D-2

OPPORTUNITY RED FLAGS: FRAUD FOR COMPANY BENEFIT

	Four Seasons	Georgia Pacific	Geotek	Giant Stores	G. L. Miller	Hochfelder	Homestake Production	Koscot—Glenn Turner	Lutz vs. First Sec. Bank	McKesson Robbins	Nat. Student Marketing	Omega-Alpha, Inc.	Penn Central	Photon, Inc.	Republic National Life	Rhode Is. Hosp. Trust	R. Hoe & Co.	S. J. Minerals	Smith vs. London Assurance	State Street Trust	Stephens Industries	Stirling Homex	Talley Industries	Ultramares	United Brands	U.S. vs. Benjamin	Vesco	Westec	Western Properties	Westgate—U.S. Financial	Wheatheart Cattle Co.	Whitaker Corp.	Yale Express	TOTAL
	x		x				x			x	x		x		x			x				x	x				x	x	x	x	x			22
	x	x		x			x			x	x		x	x								x	x					x	x	x			x	19
	x	x					x		x	x		x	x									x						x		x			x	16
	x	x		x			x							x																x				8
	x	x		x			x				x							x			x	x			x									13
							x			x					x															x				8
	x	x													x	x					x	x	x	x		x			x	x			x	20
		x									x			x				x																4
	x	x							x				x		x							x		x					x		x			15
	x						x	x					x		x			x				x	x			x				x			x	13
	x						x	x					x		x		x	x				x	x	x	x		x			x			x	21
	x		x				x				x		x		x		x					x	x	x			x			x		x	x	26
	x					x					x		x	x	x	x	x					x	x	x		x	x	x	x	x				27
	x						x				x		x	x	x	x	x					x	x	x		x		x			x			22
												x		x												x								6
	x	x		x			x				x		x		x	x	x					x	x	x		x		x	x	x	x			27
13	**7**	**1**	**4**	**2**	**1**	**10**	**1**	**3**	**5**	**11**	**2**	**10**	**4**	**9**	**4**	**3**	**4**	**0**	**1**	**4**	**13**	**9**	**7**	**0**	**7**	**3**	**9**	**5**	**10**	**3**	**1**	**0**	

TABLE D-2 Cont'd.

Personal Characteristic	Allied Crude Vegetable Oil	Ampex	Baltimore Fed. Credit	Barchris	Beardsley vs. Ernst	Beverly Hills Bankcorp	Bille Sol Estes	Black Watch Farms, Inc.	Cenco	CIT Financial	Cobuild	Continental Vending	Cosmopolitan Invst. Funding	Craig vs. Angon	Croissant vs. Watrud	Equity Funding	Essley Shirt Co.	Firestone Group Ltd.	Fisco	Four Seasons
1. Low moral character	×	×	×	×			×	×			×	×			×	×		×		×
2. Rationalizer of contradictory behavior																×				
3. Lacks a strong code of ethics	×					×	×	×								×				
4. A "wheeler-dealer"	×	×					×	×				×				×				×
5. Lacks stability																×				
6. Strong desire to beat system																				
7. Criminal or questionable background	×				×			×				×	×		×					
8. Poor credit rating or financial status																				
TOTAL	4	2	1	1	1	1	3	4	0	0	1	3	1	0	2	5	0	1	0	2

TABLE D-3
PERSONAL CHARACTERISTIC RED FLAGS

Table showing characteristic-by-company matrix (reconstructed from a rotated table). Company names are row labels; eight unlabeled data columns carry the "×" marks, with per-company totals in the TOTAL column and column totals in the bottom row.

Company									TOTAL
Georgia Pacific	×								1
Geotek	×								1
Giant Stores									0
G. L. Miller									0
Hochfelder	×								1
Homestake Production	×		×	×			×		4
Koscot—Glenn Turner				×					1
Lutz vs. First Sec. Bank	×								1
McKesson Robbins	×	×	×	×	×		×	×	7
Nat. Student Marketing	×			×					2
Omega-Alpha, Inc.							×		1
Penn Central							×		1
Photon, Inc.									0
Republic National Life				×					1
Rhode Is. Hosp. Trust									0
R. Hoe & Co.									0
S. J. Minerals	×			×					2
Smith vs. London Assurance	×								1
State Street Trust									0
Stephens Industries									0
Stirling Homex	×			×	×		×		4
Talley Industries					×				1
Ultramares	×								1
United Brands									0
U.S. vs. Benjamin	×		×	×			×		4
Vesco	×		×						2
Westec				×					1
Western Properties									0
Westgate—U.S. Financial	×	×	×	×			×		5
Wheatheart Cattle Co.		×							1
Whitaker Corp.									0
Yale Express	×			×				×	3
Column Totals	25	2	11	24	3	1	12	1	

TABLE D-3 Cont'd.

250

Individuals Against the Company	Allied Crude Vegetable Oil	Ampex	Baltimore Fed. Credit	Barchris	Beardsley vs. Ernst	Beverly Hills Bankcorp	Bille Sol Estes	Black Watch Farms, Inc.	Cenco	CIT Financial	Cobuild	Continental Vending	Cosmopolitan Invst. Funding	Craig vs. Angon	Croissant vs. Watrud	Equity Funding	Essley Shirt Co.	Firestone Group Ltd.	Fisco	Four Seasons
1. High personal debts or financial losses	x				x		x	x				x								x
2. Inadequate incomes	x																			
3. Living beyond one's means	x		x		x			x							x	x				x
4. Extensive stock market or other speculation	x							x				x								x
5. Excessive gambling																				x
6. Involvement with members of the opposite sex	x														x	x				
7. Excessive use of alcohol or drugs																x				
8. Undue family community, or social expectations	x							x		x						x				
9. Perceived inequities in the organization		x														x				
10. Corporate or peer group pressures		x														x				x
TOTAL	6	2	1	0	2	0	1	4	0	1	0	2	0	0	2	6	0	0	0	5

TABLE D-4

SITUATIONAL PRESSURE RED FLAGS:
FRAUD FOR PERSONAL BENEFIT

Georgia Pacific	Geotek	Giant Stores	G. L. Miller	Hochfelder	Homestake Production	Koscot — Glenn Turner	Lutz vs. First Sec. Bank	McKesson Robbins	Nat. Student Marketing	Omega-Alpha, Inc.	Penn Central	Photon, Inc.	Republic National Life	Rhode Is. Hosp. Trust	R. Hoe & Co.	S. J. Minerals	Smith vs. London Assurance	State Street Trust	Stephens Industries	Stirling Homex	Talley Industries	Ultramares	United Brands	U.S. vs. Benjamin	Vesco	Westec	Western Properties	Westgate — U.S. Financial	Wheatheart Cattle Co.	Whitaker Corp.	Yale Express	TOTAL
				x											x					x					x							10
					x																				x							3
				x	x	x		x	x		x									x									x			15
x								x			x															x						8
											x														x							3
								x			x																					5
																																1
											x									x	x		x							x	x	10
								x																	x							4
								x							x					x	x		x		x				x	x		11
1	0	0	0	2	2	1	0	5	1	0	5	0	0	0	2	0	0	0	0	4	2	0	2	0	5	1	0	0	2	2	1	

TABLE D-4 Cont'd.

Individuals Against the Company	Allied Crude Vegetable Oil	Ampex	Baltimore Fed. Credit	Barchris	Beardsley vs. Ernst	Beverly Hills Bankcorp	Bille Sol Estes	Black Watch Farms, Inc.	Cenco	CIT Financial	Cobuild	Continental Vending	Cosmopolitan Invst. Funding	Craig vs. Angon	Croissant vs. Watrud	Equity Funding	Essley Shirt Co.	Firestone Group Ltd.	Fisco
1. Familiarity with operations (including coverup capabilities) and in a position of trust	×	×	×	×	×	×		×	×	×		×	×	×	×	×			
2. A firm in which there is too much trust in key employees	×	×	×	×								×				×			
3. Close association with suppliers & other key people	×			×	×		×	×			×	×				×			
4. A firm which does not inform employees about rules and discipline of fraud perpetrators					×											×			
5. Lengthy tenure in key jobs	×		×	×					×			×				×	×		
6. Failure to use adequate personnel screening policies in hiring																×			
7. A firm which does not maintain accurate personnel records of dishonest acts or disciplinary actions																×			
8. A firm which does not require executive disclosures and examinations		×											×	×					
9. A firm which has a dishonest or unethical management	×	×		×	×		×	×	×			×	×			×			×
10. A firm which has a dominant top management (one or two individuals)	×	×		×	×	×	×	×	×			×	×			×		×	
11. A firm which is always operating on a crisis basis	×			×						×						×			
12. A firm which pays no attention to details	×	×																	
13. A firm where there are low interpersonal relationships and/or morale		×														×			
14. A firm which has a lack of internal security	×																		
TOTAL	9	6	4	7	5	2	3	4	4	2	1	7	4	1	2	11	1	1	1

TABLE D-5
OPPORTUNITY RED FLAGS

	Four Seasons	Georgia Pacific	Geotek	Giant Stores	G. L. Miller	Hochfelder	Homestake Production	Koscot—Glenn Turner	Lutz vs. First Sec. Bank	McKesson Robbins	Nat. Student Marketing	Omega-Alpha, Inc.	Penn Central	Photon, Inc.	Republic National Life	Rhode Is. Hosp. Trust	R. Hoe & Co.	S. J. Minerals	Smith vs. London Assurance	State Street Trust	Stephens Industries	Stirling Homex	Talley Industries	Ultramares	United Brands	U.S. vs. Benjamin	Vesco	Westec	Western Properties	Westgate—U.S. Financial	Wheatheart Cattle Co.	Whitaker Corp.	Yale Express	TOTAL
	x	x	x	x		x	x		x	x	x	x	x	x	x		x	x	x			x				x		x	x	x	x		x	44
		x		x		x			x	x			x									x						x		x	x		x	16
	x			x		x	x		x	x	x		x	x	x	x	x	x				x						x	x	x	x		x	30
																																		2
	x			x		x	x				x	x																						12
				x						x																								3
										x																								2
	x					x	x		x				x			x	x											x		x	x			12
	x	x		x		x	x		x	x	x		x		x	x	x	x				x	x	x		x		x		x	x		x	32
	x	x	x	x		x	x		x	x	x		x		x					x		x	x		x	x		x	x	x	x		x	32
			x												x							x					x							7
										x	x	x	x		x	x									x									7
													x																				x	4
																																		1
TOTAL	6	4	3	8	0	6	5	0	5	9	6	2	8	2	5	2	5	3	1	2	0	6	2	3	2	3	2	6	1	6	4	0	6	

TABLE D-5 Cont'd.

254

Bibliography

Akers, R. L., *Deviant Behavior*, Belmont, CA, Woodsworth Publishing Co., Inc., 1973.

Anderson, G. S., "Computer Manipulation Robs Our Firms of Millions of Dollars a Year," *Management World*, (July 1977):7.

Arens, A. and J. K. Loebbecke, *Auditing: An Integrated Approach*, Englewood Cliffs, NJ, Prentice-Hall, 1976.

Ash, P., "The Validation of an Instrument to Predict the Likelihood of Employee Theft," *Proceeding of the 78th Annual Convention of the American Psychological Association*, Washington, D. C., The American Psychological Association, 1970, pp. 579-580.

Ash, P., "Screening Employment Applicant for Attitudes Toward Theft," *Journal of Applied Psychology*, 55, No. 2, 1971, pp. 161-164.

Ash, P., "The Assessment of Honesty in Employment," *South African Journal of Psychology*, No. 6, 1976, pp. 68-79.

AICPA, *Statement on Auditing Standards No. 6*, New York, NY, 1975.

AICPA, *Statement on Auditing Standards No. 16*, New York, NY, 1977.

Barnett, C., "Turning the Pros into Cons," *PSA California Magazine*, May, 1978, pp. 62-66.

Baumhart, R. C., "How Ethical are Businessmen?" *Harvard Business Review*, July/August, 1961, pp. 6-9, 156-176.

Bechtold, M. L., "Validation of the K.D. Scale and Check List as Predictors of Delinquent Proneness," *Journal of Experimental Education*, 32, 1964, pp. 413-416.

Bloch, H. A. and G. Geis, *Man, Crime and Society: The Forms of Criminal Behavior*, New York, NY, Random House, 1962.

Blustein, P., "Richard Marx: A Crook's Best Friend is His Lawyer," *Forbes*, May 1, 1978, pp. 70-72.

Brief, R. P., "The Accountants' Responsibility for Disclosing Bribery: A Historical Note," *The Accounting Historian's Journal*, Fall, 1977, pp. 97-100.

Burma, J. H., "Self-Tattooing Among Delinquents: A Research Note," *Sociology and Social Research*, 43, 1959, pp. 341-345.

Burgess, R. L. and R. L. Akers, "A Differential Association-Reinforcement Theory of Criminal Behavior," *Social Problems*, 14, 1966, pp. 128-147.

Burnstein, J., "Not So Petty Larceny," *Harvard Business Review*, 37, May/June, 1959, pp. 72-78.

Burton, R. B., "Generality of Honesty Reconsidered," *Psychological Review*, 70, No. 6, 1963, pp. 481-499.

Business Week, October 28, 1972, p. 90.

Business Week, February 6, 1978, pp. 100-101.

Cardoso, B., "I Led 66,000 Lives—The Adventures of Equity Al Green and His Silent Partner in Crime—IBM 360," *Rolling Stone*, May 9, 1974, pp. 50-52.

Carmichael, D. R., "Carmichael Cites 'Red Flags' for Fraud Prevention," *Journal of Accountancy*, June, 1975, pp. 16-18.

Carmichael, D. R. and J. J. Willingham, *Perspectives in Auditing*, New York, NY, McGraw-Hill, 1975.

Carroll, A. B., "Managerial Ethics: A Post-Watergate View," *Business Horizons*, April, 1975, pp. 75-80.

Carson, C. R., *Managing Employee Honesty*, Los Angeles, CA, Security World Publishing Co., 1977.

Catlett, G. R., "Relationship of Auditing Standards to Detection of Fraud," *Arthur Andersen/University of Kansas Symposium on Auditing Problems*, Lawrence, KS, 1974, pp. 47-56.

Clarke, W. V., and K. R. Hasler, "Differentiation of Criminals and Non-Criminals with a Self-Concept Measure," *Psychological Reports*, 20, 1967, pp. 623-637.

Comer, M. J., *Corporate Fraud*, Maidenhead, Berkshire, England, McGraw-Hill Book Company (UK) Limited, 1975.

Coopers & Lybrand, "Danger Signals of Improper Practice," (Excerpt from Newsletter (Coopers & Lybrand), April, 1977), *CPA Journal*, August, 1977, pp. 76-77.

Cressey, D. R., "The Criminal Violation of Financial Trust," *American Sociological Review*, 15, December, 1950, pp. 738-743.

Cressey, D. R., "Why Do Trusted People Commit Fraud? A Social-Psychological Study of Defalcators," *Journal of Accountancy*, November, 1951, pp. 576-581.

Cressey, D. R., *Other People's Money: The Social Psychology of Embezzlement*, New York, NY, The Free Press, 1953, p. 30.

Crime in Service Industries, U. S. Department of Commerce Domestic and International Business Administration, U. S. Government Printing Office, Washington, D. C., 1977.

Curtis, S. J., *Modern Retail Security*, Charles C. Thomas, Springfield, IL, 1960.

DeFleur, M. L. and R. Quinney, "A Reformulation of Sutherland's Differential Association Theory and a Strategy for Empirical Verification," *Journal of Research in Crime and Delinquency*, 3, 1966, pp. 36-44.

Degouw, C., "Data Processing Crimes," *EDPACS*, January, 1978, pp. 1-8.

DeMarco, V., "How Internal Auditors Can Help CPAs Stamp Out Illegal Acts," *Internal Auditor*, February, 1978, pp. 60, 62, 64.

DiTullio, B., *Horizons in Clinical Criminology*, Fred B. Rothman & Co., Littleton, CO, 1969.

Edelhertz, H., *The Nature, Impact and Prosecution of White-Collar Crime*, Washington, D. C., National Institute of Law Enforcement and Criminal Justice, 1970.

Ellison, R., "The Changing Face of 'Fraudsman,'" *CPA Journal*, January, 1976, pp. 5-6.

Eysenck, S. B. G., J. Rust, and H. J. Eysenck, "Personality and the Classification of Adult Offenders," *British Journal of Criminology*, April, 1977, pp. 169-179.

Ferguson, R. J., Jr., *The Scientific Informer*, Springfield, IL, Charles C. Thomas, 1971.

Freed, R., "Computer Fraud—A Management Trap," *Business Horizons*, June, 1969, pp. 25-30.

Freedman, M. S., "A Primer on Fraud and Embezzlement," *Management Accounting*, October, 1973, pp. 35-40.

Forbes, "Four Seasons: A Great Story With an Unhappy Ending," July 15, 1970, p. 55.

Foster, W., "Related Party Transactions—Some Considerations," *CPA Journal*, May, 1975, pp. 15-19.

Geis, G., *White Collar Criminal: The Offender in Business and the Professions*, New York, NY, Atherton Press, 1968.

Gibbons, D. C., "Criminality Among 'Respectable Citizens,'" (From *Society, Crime and Criminal Careers*, 2nd Edition), Englewood Cliffs, NJ, Prentice-Hall, Inc., 1973, pp. 324-353.

Gibson, H. B., "The Validation of a Technique for Measuring Delinquent Association by Means of Vocabulary," *British Journal of Social and Clinical Psychology*, 5, 1966, pp. 190-195.

Gilson, M., "Computer Assisted Fraud," *Data Management*, April, 1975, p. 22-23.

Glick, R. G. and R. S. Newsom, *Fraud Investigation—Fundamentals for Police*, Springfield, IL, Charles C. Thomas, 1974.

Goring, C., "The English Convict: A Statistical Study," London, His Majesty's Stationary Office, 1913.

Gorrill, B. E., *How to Prevent Losses and Improve Profits with Effective Personnel Security Procedures*, Homewood, IL, Dow Jones—Irwin, 1974.

Gottheimer, D., "Those Hidden 'Opportunities' for Computer Crime," *Administrative Management*, January, 1978, pp. 65-66, 68, 72, 74, 76, 78.

Gough, H. G., "Theory and Measurement of Socialization," *Journal of Consulting Psychology*, 24, 1960, pp. 23-30.

Gough, H. G., "Cross-Cultural Validation of a Measure of Asocial Behavior," *Psychological Reports*, 17, 1965, pp. 379-387.

Gough, H. G., and D. R. Peterson, "The Indentification and Measurement of Predispositional Factors in Crime and Delinquency," *Journal of Consulting Psychology*, 16, 1952, pp. 207-212.

Haas, P. C., Jr., "Closing the Door on Internal Bank Fraud," *The Personnel Administrator*, November, 1978, pp. 45-50.

Hartshorne, H. and M. A. May, *Studies in the Nature of Character, Vol. 1, Studies in Deceit*, New York, NY, Macmillian Publishing Co., Inc., 1928.

Hathaway, S. R. and E. D. Monachesi (eds.), *Analyzing and Predicting Delinquency with the MMPI*, Minneapolis, MN, University of Minnesota Press, 1953.

Hayes, C. D., Research Branch, *Texas Dept. of Corrections*, (Personal Correspondence), 1978.

Hernon, F. E., "Industrial Purchasing Safeguards: Reducing Criminal Frauds," *Financial Executive*, May, 1976, pp. 20-25.

Herzberg, F., Panel Discussion at a Conference on White-Collar Crime held at Brigham Young University, 1976.

Holmes, G., "Roadships, Ltd.—Yet Another Lesson for Auditors," *Accountancy*, December, 1976, pp. 78-83.

Hooton, E. A., *The American Criminal: An Anthropological Study*, New York, NY, Greenwood Press, 1939.

Horvath, F. E. and J. E. Reid, "The Rehability of Polygraph Examiner Diagnosis of Truth and Deception," *Journal of Criminal Law, Criminology, and Police Science*, 62(2), 276-281, 1971.

Howell, R. J., I. R. Payne and A. V. Roe, "The Bipolar Psychological Inventory," Orem, UT, Diagnostic Specialists, 1972.

Hunter, F. E. and P. Ash, "The Accuracy and Consistency of Polygraph Examiners' Diagnoses," *Journal of Police Science and Administration*, 3, 1973, pp. 370-375.

Jaspan, N., *Mind Your Own Business*, Englewood Cliffs, NJ, Prentice-Hall, 1974.

Jaspan, N., "Problem—People—Prevention," *National Public Accountant*, May, 1972, pp. 27-33.

Jefferey, W. J., "The Forty Thieves," FBI Law Enforcement Bulletin (excerpt), Baltimore, IN, 39, No. 7, pp. 16-19, 29-30, and 39, No. 8, pp. 21-25, 29-30, 1970.

Jensen, M., and W. H. Meckling, "Theory of the Firm Managerial Behavior, Agency Costs and Ownership Structure," *Journal of Financial Economics*, October, 1976, pp. 305-360.

Jones, J. W., Employee Deviance: Attitudinal Correlates of Theft and On-the-Job Alcohol Abuse. Submitted for Publication to the *Journal of the American Criminal Justice Association*, 1980.

Kapnick, H., "Management Fraud and the Independent Auditor," *Journal of Commercial Bank Lending*, December, 1975, pp. 20-30.

Kapnick, H., "Responsibility Detection in Management Fraud," *CPA Journal*, May, 1976, pp. 19-23.

Kelley, C. M., "White-Collar Crime," Testimony of Clarence M. Kelley, Director, Federal Bureau of Investigation, Before the House Subcommittee on Appropriations, February 20, 1976.

Kintzele, P. L. and K. D. Kintzele, "Fraud: Its Prevention and Detection," *The National Public Accountant*, April, 1976, pp. 11-16.

Klein, D. J. and M. L. Densmore, "Improving Internal Control to Curb White-Collar Crime," *The National Public Accountant*, November, 1977, pp. 11-16.

Krause, S., "Business Frauds: Their Perpetration, Detection and Redress," *The National Public Accountant*, November, 1965, pp. 8-34.

Lane, R. E., "Why Businessmen Violate the Law," *Journal of Criminal Law, Criminology and Police Science*, July/August, 1953, pp. 151-165.

LaPiere, R. T. and R. Farnsworth, Social Psychology, New York, NY, McGraw-Hill, 1949.

Lebowitz, H. M., U. S. Bureau of Prisons (Personal Correspondence), 1978.

Leibholz, S. W. and L. D. Wilson, *User's Guide to Computer Crime, Its Commission, Detection and Prevention*, Radnor, PA, Chilton Book Company, 1974.

Levens, G. E., "101 British White-Collar Criminals," *New Society*, March 26, 1964, pp. 6-8.

Loeffler, Robert M., *Report of the Trustee of Equity Funding Corporation of America*, October 31, 1974.

Lillian, D., *Corporate Treasurer's and Controller's Encyclopedia*, Englewood Cliffs, NJ, Prentice-Hall, 1968.

Littrell, Earl K., "Creative Accounting—Assets-for-Stock: Now You See 'Em, Now You . . . ," *Management Accounting*, February, 1980.

Lottier, S. F., "Tension Theory of Criminal Behavior," *American Sociological Review*, 7, December, 1942, pp. 840-848.

Lykken, D. T., "Psychology and the Lie Detector Industry," *American Psychologist*, October, 1974, pp. 725-739.

Mangold, K. M., "Comparison of Delinquents and Non-Delinquents on IES Test," *Perceptual and Motor Skill*, 22, 1965, pp. 317-318.

Mannerheim, H., "Our Criminogenic Society III: White-Collar and Other 'Non-Working-Class' Crimes," *Comparative Criminology*, 2, ed. H. Mannerheim, London, 1965, pp. 469-498.

Megargee, E. E., "Undercontrolled and Overcontrolled Personality Types in Extreme Antisocial Aggression," *Psychological Monographs*, 80, No. 3, 1966.

Meyers, E., "Computer Criminals Beware," *Datamation*, December, 1975, pp. 105-107.

Middlebrook, P. N., *Social Psychology and Modern Life*, New York, NY, Alfred A. Knopf, 1974.

Miller, C., "Union Dime Picks up the Pieces in $1.5 Million Embezzlement Case," *Bank Systems and Equipment*, May, 1973, pp. 34-35, 92.

Miller, J. N., "Buying and Selling at the Pentagon," *The Reader's Digest*, April, 1978, pp. 115-120.

Morgenson, D. F., "White-Collar Crime and the Violation of Trust," *Personnel Journal*, March, 1975, pp. 154-155, 176.

Morris, A., "Criminals of the Upper World," *Criminology*, ed. A. Morris, New York, NY, 1935, pp. 152-158.

Nettler, G., "Embezzlement Without Problems," *British Journal of Criminology*, 14, No. 1, 1974, pp. 70-77.

Nolan, J., "FBI Agent Accountants Intensify Campaign Against 'White-Collar' Crime," *Journal of Accountancy*, October, 1974, pp. 26, 28, 30.

Norman, A., "Computer Frauds—Are They a Manageable Risk?" *Accountancy*, October, 1976, pp. 78-79, 81.

Nycum, S. H., "Computer Abuses Raise New Legal Problems," *American Bar Association Journal*, April, 1975, pp. 444-448.

Parker, D. B., "Further Comment on the Equity Funding Insurance Fraud Case," *EDPACS*, January, 1975, p. 16.

Parker, D. B., *Ethical Conflicts in Computer Science and Technology*, Montvale, NJ, AFIPS Press, 1978.

Pecar, J., "White-Collar Crime and Social Control," *International Journal of Criminology and Penology*, May, 1975, pp. 183-199.

Podgus, C., "Outwitting the Computer Swindler," *Computer Decision*, September, 1973, pp. 12-16.

Porteus, S. D., "Q-Scores, Temperament, and Delinquency," *Journal of Social Psychology*, 21, 1945, pp. 81-103.

Porteus, S. D., *Porteus Maze Test: Fifty Years' Application*, Palo Alto, CA, Pacific Books, 1968.

Prather, J., "Post-Release Success of White-Collar Offenders," Office of Research, Washington D. C., U. S. Bureau of Prisons, 1977.

Quinney, E. R., "Occupational Structure and Criminal Behavior: Prescription Violation by Retail Pharmacists," *Social Problems*, 11, (Fall 1963) pp. 179-185.

Quinney, E. R., "The Study of White Collar Crime: Toward a Reorientation in Theory and Research," *Journal of Criminal Law, Criminology and Police Science*, June, 1964, pp. 208-214.

Rauchlin, M. S., "Managing Your Practice—How to Tell Your Clients that Fraud is Their Responsibility," *The Practical Accountant*, May/June, 1977, pp. 34-35.

Reasons, C. E. (ed.), *The Criminologist—Crime and the Criminal*, Santa Monica, CA, Goodyear Publishing Co., 1974.

Reid, J. E., *The Reid Report*, Chicago, IL, John E. Reid and Associates, 1967.

Reid, J. E., and F. E. Inbau, *Truth and Deception: The Polygraph ('Lie Detector') Technique*, Baltimore, MD, Wilkins and Wilkins, 1966.

Reimer, S., "Embezzlement: Pathological Basis," *Journal of Criminal Law and Criminology*, 32, November/December, 1941, pp. 411-423.

Rice, B., "The New Truth Machines," *Psychology Today*, June, 1978, pp. 61-78.

Robertson, W., "Those Daring Young Con Men of Equity Funding," *Fortune*, August, 1973, pp. 81-85, 120.

Robin, G. D., "Employees as Offenders: A Sociological Analysis of Occupational Crime," Ph.D. Thesis, University of Pennsylvania, 1965.

Romney M. and W. S. Albrecht, "The Use of Investigative Agencies by Auditors," *Journal of Accountancy*, October, 1979, pp. 61-66.

Rose, N., *Balance Sheet Offenses*, Washington, D.C., Law Enforcement Administration Association, 1975.

Russell, H., "Facing the Problem—Fraud," *Internal Auditor*, July/August, 1975, pp. 13-23.

Shapiro, S., *Background Paper on White-Collar Crime—Considerations of Conceptualization and Future Research*, Law Enforcement Assistance Administration, Washington, D. C., National Institute of Law Enforcement and Criminal Justice, 1976.

Sheldon, W. H., S. S. Stevens, and W. B. Tucker, *Varieties of Human Physique*, New York, NY, Harper and Row, 1940.

Simon, R. J., "Female Felons," *Human Behavior*, November, 1978, p. 12.

Sneath, C., "An Auditing Viewpoint," *Accountant*, October 2, 1975, pp. 388-391.

Spencer, J. C., "White-Collar Crime," *(From Criminology in Transition*, T. Grygier, H. Jones, and J. C. Spencer (eds.)), London, U.K., Travistock Publications, 1965, pp. 251-264.

Steffen, R., "How I Embezzled $1.5 Million . . . And Nearly Got Away With It," *Bank Systems and Equipment*, June, 1974, pp. 24-28.

Stone, J., "Professional Deprivation Tied to DP Crime?" *Computerworld*, January 23, 1978, p. 21.

Stone, J. and I. Mason, "DP Crooks Going Unnoticed, Undiscouraged," *Computerworld*, January 16, 1978, p. 17.

Sutherland, E. H., "Crime of Corporations," *In the Sutherland Papers*, (eds.) A. Cohen, A. Lindesmith, and K. Schuessler, Bloomington, IN, Indiana University Press, 1956.

Sutherland, E. H., *On Analyzing Crime*, Karl Schuessler (ed.), Chicago, IL, University of Chicago Press, 1973.

Sutherland, E. H. and D. R. Cressey, *Criminology*, 10th ed., Philadelphia, PA, Lippincott, 1978.

Taylor, A. J. W., "Tattooing Among Male and Female Offenders of Different Ages in Different Types of Institutions," *Genetic Psychology Monographs*, 81, 1970, pp. 81-119.

Terris, W., Attitudinal Correlates of Theft, Violence, and Drug-Use, Proceedings of the Seventeenth Interamerican Congress of Psychology, 1979. (In Press).

Touche Ross and Co., "Management Involvement in Material Transactions," *Audit Technical Letter 149*, August 1, 1974.

U. S. Chamber of Commerce, *Crime In Service Industries*, Washington, D. C., Government Printing Office, 1977.

U. S. Chamber of Commerce, *Handbook on White-Collar Crime: Everyone's Problem, Everyone's Loss*, Washington, D. C., Government Printing Office, 1974.

U. S. Fidelity and Guaranty Company, *The Forty Thieves*, 1970.

U. S. News & World Report, "Compulsive Gambling: A Spreading Epidemic," January 28, 1980, p. 73.

Vold, G. B., "Theoretical Criminology," New York, NY, Oxford University Press, 1958, pp. 4-8.

Waller, R. R., "Computer Fraud," *The Accountant*, October 2, 1975, pp. 392-393.

Wall Street Journal, "Black Watch Farms Collapse Investigated; Fraud, $3.2 Million Embezzlement Alleged," June 1, 1973a.

Wall Street Journal, "Five Top Officers at Weis Securities Indicted for Fraud," July 17, 1973b.

Wall Street Journal, "Residex Sues Figures in Co-Build and Other Facts of Stock Sale," August 7, 1973c.

Wall Street Journal, "Allen & Co., Inc., Laventhol Cited in Security Fraud," June 12, 1974a.

Wall Street Journal, "Beverly Hills Bancorp, Others Charged with Securities Law Violation by SEC," August 7, 1974b.

Wall Street Journal, "Fisco to Post '73 Loss of $26.2 Million; Sues Auditor on '72 Results," May 10, 1974c.

Wall Street Journal, "Eight Ex-Officials of Franklin National Indicted by U. S. Jury in Bank's Collapse," August 13, 1975a.

Wall Street Journal, "Fraud Schemes Caused T. P. Richardson to Fail, Brokerage Firm Receiver Says," July 2, 1975b.

Wall Street Journal, "Omega-Alpha, Ex-Chief Being Accused by SEC of Fraud in Sale of Unit's Notes," February 10, 1975c.

Wall Street Journal, "Ex-REA Express Officials Tell of Schemes to Loot the Concern as It Was Collapsing," September 27, 1978a.

Wall Street Journal, "Mattel Ex-Chief, Others Indicted on Fraud Counts," February 17, 1978b.

Wall Street Journal, "Overdriven Execs, Some Managers Cut Corners to Achieve High Corporate Goals," November 8, 1979a.

Wall Street Journal, "SEC Censures Touche Ross Over Auditing of Defunct Giant Stores' Fiscal Report," June 28, 1979b.

Wall Street Journal, "Seven Ex-Officials of Cenco are Indicted on Counts of Inflating Firm's Inventories," April 25, 1979c.

Wall Street Journal, "Huge Grain Scandal Has Iowa Farmers Shaking Their Heads," March 12, 1980.

Weinstein, E., "A Time of Travail and Challenge," *CPA Journal,* December, 1974, pp. 29-31.

Weiss, H., "Rebuttal to Equity Funding Implications," *EDPACS,* October, 1974, pp. 8-11.

Woolf, E., "Lessons of Equity Funding," *Accountancy,* January, 1977, pp. 30-40.

Yochelson, S. and S. E. Samenow, *The Criminal Personality. Vol. 1: A Profile for Change.* New York, NY, Jason Aronson, 1976.

Zeitlin, Lawrence R., "A Little Larceny Can Do a Lot for Employee Morale," *Psychology Today,* June, 1971, pp. 22-26.

INDEX